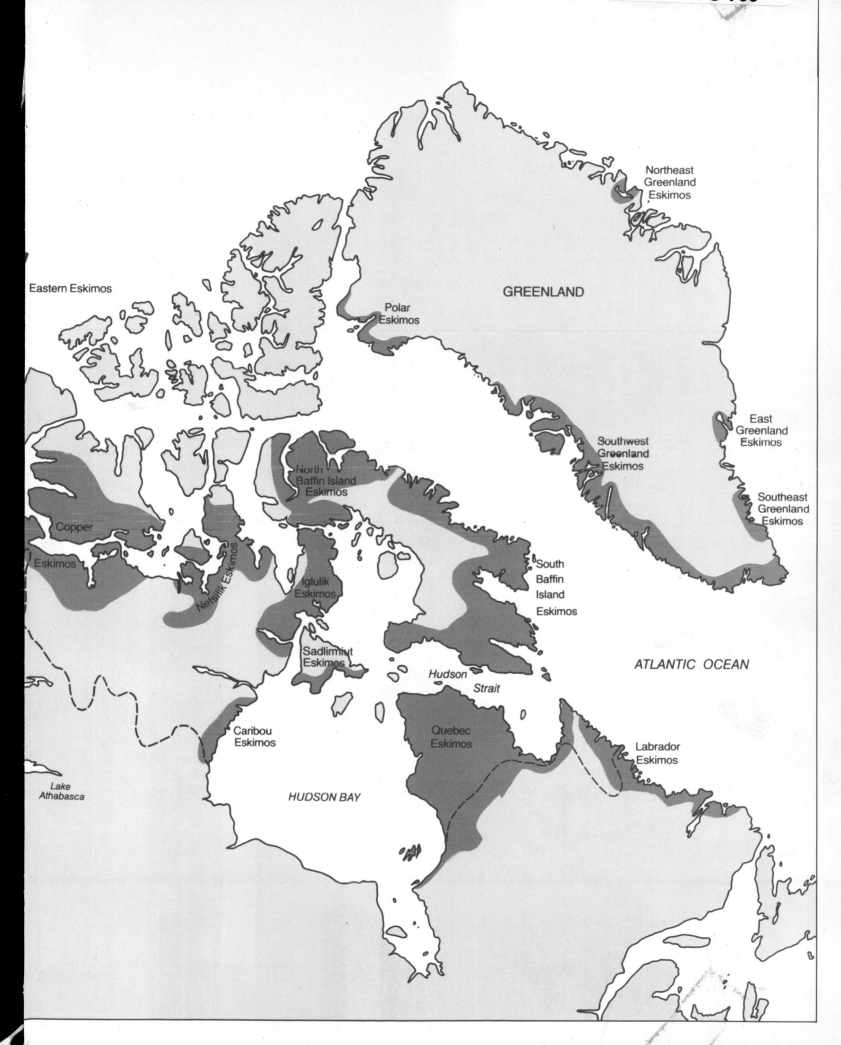

Northeast
Greenland
Eskimos

Eastern Eskimos

GREENLAND

Polar
Eskimos

East
Greenland
Eskimos

Southwest
Greenland
Eskimos

North
Baffin Island
Eskimos

Southeast
Greenland
Eskimos

Copper
Eskimos

Netsilik Eskimos

South
Baffin
Island
Eskimos

Iglulik
Eskimos

ATLANTIC OCEAN

Sadlirmiut
Eskimos

Hudson

Strait

Caribou
Eskimos

Quebec
Eskimos

Labrador
Eskimos

Lake
Athabasca

HUDSON BAY

The Eskimos

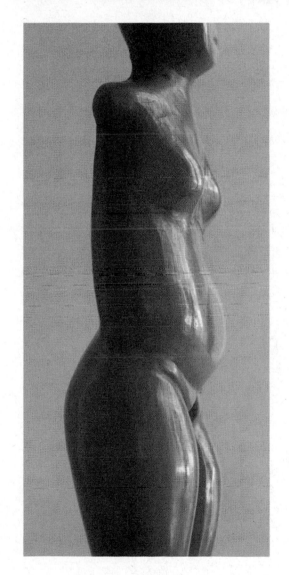

The Eskimos

Text by Ernest S. Burch, Jr
Photographs by Werner Forman

University of Oklahoma Press
Norman and London

*Half title page: Venus of the north, this armless
but otherwise realistic ivory carving of a human
female came from the Eastern Arctic. It was
worn as a pendant.*

*Title page: The waters off Southwest Greenland
rarely freeze, because of the warming influence
of the Gulf Stream, but ice does form in the calm
waters of protected bays and fiords. Frozen sea
water is initially too salty to drink, but becomes
fresh over the winter as the salt percolates
downward through the ice.*

CONTENTS

INTRODUCTION

Prince William Sound marked the deepest penetration of Eskimos into forested country. They found the region rich in sea mammals, fish and timber, but had to contend with some powerful neighbours, the Tlingit Indians of the Pacific Northwest.

Across the northern periphery of Eurasia and North America stretches an expanse of treeless country which is generally viewed as a wasteland by residents of more verdant climes. Often referred to as 'the barrens' by English-speaking peoples, this land is not truly barren in the sense of being altogether devoid of life. On the contrary, most of it is covered by grass or by tundra vegetation (grasses, lichens, mosses) and dwarf trees and shrubs, and a remarkable number of flowers return each summer to grace even the most desolate hillside. The barrens is also home to surprising numbers of animals at certain times of the year. But it does lack large woody trees, and, in general, cannot support any form of agriculture. These features have a profoundly inhibiting effect on human enterprise, and the common perception of the barrens as being a hostile environment is well founded.

People do live on the barrens nevertheless. In both the Old World and the New, most of this land has been occupied by people ever since the last ice age ended, several thousand years ago. Traditionally, in most of northern Eurasia, human occupation was only seasonal. Members of several different ethnic groups – Lapps, Samoyeds, Tungus, Yukagir – travelled on to the barrens every summer, but returned to the shelter of the forest in winter. In North America, on the other hand, much of the barrens was inhabited all year round, and by the members of a single ethnic group, the Eskimos.

Eskimos lived along the northern perimeter of the entire continent, from Greenland and Labrador, in the east, to Alaska and the eastern shores of Asia, in the west. The barrens varies considerably in extent from one portion of this vast region to another, and it disappears altogether in the extreme southwestern and southeastern sectors. In general, wherever the size of the treeless region expands, so did the size of Eskimo territory; and where it contracts, Eskimo territory did too. In areas such as southwestern Alaska and southeastern Labrador, where Eskimos lived in or near the forest, they had to compete with American Indians for land and food. This competition frequently erupted into war, an enterprise in which the Eskimos were by no means uniformly successful. On the barrens, however, Eskimos were all but unchallenged, since no other traditional North American people was able to survive without trees for more than a few months at a time. Eskimos have lived continuously in treeless country for at least 4000 years!

Just when and how the Eskimos became a distinct human population remains a mystery. Nearly as obscure is the course of events which brought them from their original state several thousand years ago to the condition in which they were first encountered by Europeans. Nevertheless, thanks to the efforts of archaeologists, at least the general outlines of Eskimo prehistory are beginning to be understood.

7

The first human inhabitants of the New World were descended from people who expanded eastward out of Asia to Alaska, thence to Canada, the continental United States, and eventually South America. This process probably began some 50,000 years ago, when the level of the ocean dropped so low that a 'land bridge' was created between Asia and North America. This expansion out of the Old World continued at a fluctuating but generally slow rate over the ensuing millennia, as ocean levels rose and fell, and as immense continental glaciers in Canada expanded and shrank.

Movement between Alaska and the continental United States was probably impossible from about 20,000 to 15,000 years ago, and it must have been very difficult for a long time before and after that. At its maximum extent the land bridge was some 1600 kilometres (990 miles) wide, but the glaciers had expanded to such an extent that movement between Alaska and the continental United States was cut off. Almost all of what is now Canada was covered by ice.

American Indians are descended from the people who were caught south of the Canadian ice sheets. Eskimos are descended from people who remained somewhere north and west of it. They were still part of the general population of Asia because the land bridge connected western and interior Alaska to Asia at the time. The ancestors of the Eskimos thus participated in the biological and cultural developments of Asia for several thousand years after the ancestors of the Indians had been entirely cut off from them. This, in essence, is why Eskimos are more Mongoloid in appearance than are American Indians.

The rising ocean again breached the land bridge about 13,000 years ago. By 10,000 years ago it had risen sufficiently for water and ice conditions in Bering Strait to begin to approximate their present condition. It is from about this time that archaeological evidence relating to the question of Eskimo origins first appears. By 6000 years ago, populations possibly ancestral to Eskimos were living in what were then the grasslands of western Alaska.

Between about 6000 and 4000 years ago Eskimo populations expanded the whole way across the top of the New World – to Greenland, in the east, and to the tip of the Aleutian Islands, in the west. Subsequent millennia saw a number of cultural efflorescences and declines, and population expansions and contractions. As might be expected of the prehistory of any people distributed over such an immense area for such a long period of time, that of the Eskimos was fairly complex.

If the Eskimos ever had a golden age, it was probably the first millennium AD. That era saw brilliant creativity in both arts and manufactures, perfection of the skills and equipment required to hunt the diverse kinds of northern animals, and significant population growth. These developments originated along the shores of the Bering Sea and Bering Strait, but they subsequently spread eastward right to the Atlantic coast, and northward into the most distant reaches of the American Arctic.

In Alaska and eastern Asia this exciting time of ferment and innovation was followed by a long period of consolidation. Having mastered techniques for dealing with the environment and with the world of the supernatural, the more westerly Eskimo groups turned their creative energies to working out arrangements for dealing with one another. War and trade, rather than subsistence and religion, became the focus of innovation and experiment.

In the Central and Eastern Arctic, the expansionary period was followed by an

The Alaska peninsula and the Aleutian Islands are dominated by a series of snow-capped volcanoes, such as Mount Iliamna. Volcanic eruptions, earthquakes and tsunamis (tidal waves) were among the natural hazards with which the inhabitants of these regions had to contend.

The great ice cap that covers the interior of Greenland reaches the sea through glaciers – moving rivers of freshwater ice. Here a small glacier cuts through the coastal mountains to deposit its burden in the sea. The floating ice in the foreground is not frozen sea water, but a number of relatively small icebergs that 'calved' from the glacier.

era of increasing cold known as 'the little ice age'. Life in these regions became progressively more difficult from about AD 1500 on, and the main cultural focus in many areas became sheer survival. Many local populations died out altogether through increasingly frequent and severe famines, and most of the others were significantly reduced in size.

When Europeans first began to acquire accurate knowledge of the North American Arctic, in the sixteenth century, the Eskimos, numbering perhaps 75,000 at the time, were thinly distributed for some 20,000 kilometres (12,000 miles) across the northern periphery of the continent. Over the next three centuries, but particularly between about 1750 and 1885, their numbers were cut drastically by European diseases. Their way of life, as an integrated whole, was largely destroyed in most areas by the early twentieth century.

The situation described in the following pages dates primarily from the early 1800s. We know how Eskimos lived then because many individual elements of their traditional culture survived beyond that time. Many others, although no longer practised or observed, were remembered by older people who conveyed part of their knowledge to ethnologists who, in turn, recorded it for posterity. This information, when combined with the eyewitness observations of contemporary explorers and with the results of archaeological research, yields a

This Greenlandic child died of unknown causes some 500 years ago. Its body was found with those of seven others, preserved through natural mummification in the desert-dry air of the far north. Such remains are just one of several forms of evidence studied for clues about how Eskimos lived in the past.

comprehensive, although regrettably incomplete, picture of the former Eskimo way of life.

Eskimos generally were Mongoloid in appearance. They had the characteristic epicanthic eye fold; a large, flat face with prominent cheekbones; straight black hair; relatively little facial or body hair; and skin that was light in colour, although readily tanned a dark brown. Their hands and feet were small but their hands tended to be well muscled. They were relatively short in most regions because of their short legs, but their long trunks gave them a comparatively tall sitting height. Before they adopted elements of a Western diet, Eskimos – especially the men – tended toward spareness. Within the Eskimo area the main visible physical variation was in head shape: in the far west they were very round-headed, but progressively less so as one moved farther east.

Culturally, regional variation was more pronounced. As Europeans gradually discovered, the people referred to indiscriminately as 'Eskimos' in fact spoke several languages, all belonging to a language family now known as 'Eskaleut'. It is believed that the languages in this family are related to some of those spoken in eastern Asia, but evidence in support of that theory is inconclusive.

The Eskaleut language family is divided into two branches, Aleut and Eskimo. Linguists believe that they have been diverging from one another for about 4000 years. The languages are so different that the two groups are normally thought of as being entirely different peoples. Those speaking languages in the former branch are 'Aleuts'; those speaking languages in the latter are 'Eskimos'. It was only after the ancient link between the two had been established that the term 'Eskaleut' was invented to indicate their prehistoric relationship. Since this book deals with the entire language family, it is technically about Eskaleuts.

There seem to have been about 14,000 speakers of Aleut languages at the time of local European contact in 1741. They lived in what is now extreme southwestern Alaska, on a portion of the Alaska peninsula, and along the entire chain of Aleutian Islands. They spoke three related languages or dialects which have been designated Eastern, Central – which is now extinct – and Western Aleut to reflect their geographic distribution. The three language groups were also characterized by differences in belief, ritual and social organization. Unfortunately, the devastation wrought by the Russians on the Aleut population was so severe, and happened so swiftly, that few details of these differences are known to us. Only the Eastern Aleuts have been described in any detail. Even there, most of the published accounts were written so long after European contact that it is difficult to know whether they refer to patterns which characterized an earlier way of life or to those which were a direct result of Russian influence.

The waters of the mighty Yukon River reach the Bering Sea through a bewildering complex of channels, having travelled some 2400 km (1500 miles) from the mountains of Yukon territory, in Canada. Every spring the river's floodwaters carry tons of silt to the ocean, and each summer millions of salmon ascend it to spawn.

The Eskimo branch of the Eskaleut language family was divided into two groups, Yupik and Inuit. In the mid-eighteenth century, the approximately 24,000 Yupik speakers lived in southcentral and southwestern Alaska, in discontinuous parts of the Asiatic coast and on St Lawrence Island in the Bering Sea. They spoke at least five different languages, which have been designated as Pacific Yupik and Central Alaskan Yupik, spoken in Alaska, and Naukanskii, Chaplinskii and Sirenikskii, spoken on the Asiatic shore of the Bering Sea and Bering Strait. Inuit, by contrast, was not divided into separate languages. Its approximately 35,000 speakers (in the late eighteenth century) were distributed the whole way from Bering Strait to eastern Greenland.

Each of the nine linguistic zones was associated with a number of other cultural differences, but the aim here is to describe patterns that were common to them all. Regional differences cannot be ignored, though, and many are quite fascinating. Where necessary, identifying labels, such as 'Aleut' or 'Pacific Eskimos' will be employed, all referring to groups identified specifically on the map on the endpapers of this book. Generally, however, it is more useful to distinguish between 'Eastern Eskimos', on the one hand, and 'Western Eskimos', on the other. The latter included all of the Aleuts, all of the Yupik Eskimos, and the Inuit-speaking Eskimos of Northwest Alaska and the Mackenzie Delta region of northwestern Canada. Their culture was strongly influenced by neighbouring Asian and American Indian cultures; indeed, in many respects it was more like the culture of the Northwest Coast Indians of British Columbia and southeastern Alaska than to that of the Eskimo-speaking peoples of eastern Canada and Greenland. The Eastern Eskimos included the balance of the Eskaleut population, which means the Inuit-speaking people of the Central and Eastern North American Arctic.

The awkward term 'Eskaleut', although technically correct, will be avoided in favour of the better-known word 'Eskimo'. 'Eskimo', curiously enough, is not an Eskimo word. Just where it originated is not certain, but according to legend it was an Algonkian Indian word meaning 'eaters of raw flesh'. Most Eskimos referred to themselves by words which meant 'human beings', or 'authentic human beings'. These designations served to differentiate them from 'Louse Nits', meaning American Indians, and from other substandard creatures who, in the Eskimo view, may have been physically similar to human beings, but who were actually inferior representatives of the animal kingdom.

The specific native word used to convey their own ethnic identity varied, not

Characteristic motifs of Old Bering Sea (AD 1–500) art embellish this 'winged object'. Long a source of mystery to archaeologists, these artefacts are now thought to have served as stabilizers on spear shafts.

only from one language to another, but also to some extent among the dialects of a single language. Thus, the Eastern Arctic form *Inuit* progressively gave way in the west to *Inummaariit, Inuvialat, Inupiat, Yuppiit, Yuppiat, Suxpiat, Yuget, Yupiget, Unangan* . . . . Clearly no native word designated more than a small portion of the overall population, which means that any term used to designate all Eskaleut groups has to be a fabrication.

In Canada, 'Inuit' has recently replaced 'Eskimo' as a general term of reference. Given the fact that the majority of Canadian Eskimos use 'Inuit' to refer to themselves, this is not unreasonable. Since the Inuit have never constituted more than sixty per cent of the total Eskimo population, however, it is misleading in the extreme to consider 'Inuit' and 'Eskimo' as equivalent terms. Since 'Eskimo' (or 'Esquimaux') has been used consistently in the West for several hundred years, and since there is no universally (or even widely) applicable native term, 'Eskimo' remains the most appropriate word to use when referring to the population as a whole.

The differences among the various Eskimo groups reflected the long period of development of the Eskimo population, its immense geographic distribution, and the pronounced environmental differences that existed between one portion of the Eskimo area and another. The climate is cold, but by no means uniformly

so. Commonly thought of as Arctic dwellers, the great majority of Eskimos actually lived south of the Arctic Circle. In fact, fully a quarter of the population lived within the same range of latitudes as those encompassing the British Isles. There is considerable climatic variation from one region to another, and the country contains practically every conceivable type of landscape.

Eskimo country is not entirely devoid of trees, but in many sectors the only wood available was driftwood, and a few areas lacked even that. The paucity of vegetable resources meant that Eskimos had to derive most of their sustenance from fish and game. The fauna of the Eskimo area included several varieties of hair seal and whale, and the walrus, while sea lions, fur seals and sea otters joined the list in the Aleutian Island and Pacific Eskimo sectors. Caribou (wild reindeer), absent in the Aleutians, were the most important land animals almost

The Yukon-Kuskokwim Delta covers a vast area in southwestern Alaska. Viewed as a barren waste by Westerners, it was known to the Eskimos as a land of plenty. Millions of fish filled its rivers, huge numbers of ducks and geese nested on the shores of its countless sloughs and ponds, and herds of caribou migrated across its surface. This picture shows a maze of old river channels that have been filled with silt and covered with grass. The dark green consists of spruce trees growing on the old river banks and well-drained ridges rising above the surrounding plain.

everywhere else. Polar bears, grizzly bears and musk oxen were abundant in some regions, as were a variety of fur-bearing animals, such as foxes, wolves and wolverines, and small game, such as hares and ground-squirrels. Many species of migratory waterfowl and cliff-dwelling birds come north in incredible numbers in summer in many regions, but the only terrestrial bird of any significance in most areas was the small, quail-like ptarmigan. Several varieties of fish complete the basic list of Arctic fauna, including several species of whitefish and trout in the lakes and rivers, herring, smelt, capelin and two or three species of small cod in the sea, and charr and salmon moving between fresh water and salt.

The country occupied by Western Eskimos was richer in natural resources than that inhabited by their Eastern kinsmen. In particular, it was more generously endowed with useful vegetable products and fish. These differences were

The great barrenlands of northern Canada stretch westward from Hudson Bay. Scoured by the continental glaciers of the Pleistocene Epoch, and exposed to some of the worst winds the Arctic climate can produce, this region is the least productive sector of the entire Eskimo world.

reflected in the respective population densities of the two regions. Although they occupied three-quarters of the entire Eskimo area, the Eastern Eskimos constituted less than a third of the total population. They are, nonetheless, the 'typical' Eskimos described in Western literature. A less biased presentation must devote greater attention to the Western Eskimos who, in a statistical sense at least, were more representative of Eskimos in general than were their Eastern counterparts.

Western Eskimo territory was not only richer in natural resources than that of the Eastern Eskimos, it was also the geographic focus of much higher levels of culture contact and exchange with other groups. The combination of higher population density and greater cultural stimulation produced in the Western Eskimos both greater diversity and greater complexity in practically all areas of life than occurred in the east.

Eastern Eskimos were the first to experience direct contact with Europeans, however. The very earliest of these encounters occurred around the end of the first millennium AD during the Norse exploration and settlement of Greenland and the western North Atlantic. Unfortunately, the Norse colonists died out without leaving any useful records of these contacts. In the sixteenth century, in southwestern Greenland, Labrador and Baffin Island, European fishermen and whalers and a few explorers again encountered Eskimos, but their meetings were brief and superficial. It was only in the early eighteenth century, when more extensive exploration began, that some reasonably accurate information about Eskimo life was obtained. Tragically, more sustained contact with Europeans also resulted in a series of catastrophic epidemics of European diseases, such as smallpox and measles. By the end of the eighteenth century the populations of Greenland and Labrador had declined significantly.

Direct contact between Europeans and Western Eskimos began in the first half of the eighteenth century, when Russians pushed eastward to the Bering Sea and the north Pacific. Intent on conquest, the Russians were prepared to fight anyone who stood in their way. The natives they encountered in southern Alaska, both

Eskimos reached the shores of Greenland some 4500 years ago, and resided there for a prolonged period. For reasons yet unknown, they died out or abandoned the country during the first millenium AD. When Norse colonists arrived around AD 1000, they had the country to themselves and founded two settlements. But when Eskimos returned a few centuries later, they proved better able to cope with the deteriorating climate than the Norse; it was then the Europeans' turn to disappear, leaving behind remains of what once had been a thriving colony.

Indians and Eskimos, were formidable warriors and not easily subdued, but the combined effect of superior weapons and newly imported diseases ultimately gave the victory to the Russians.

Europeans moved, usually peacefully, from both the east and west toward the centre of the Eskimo area. Explorers usually led the way, followed by traders and missionaries, and eventually by others. As they proceeded, the diseases they brought with them took a terrible toll of one Eskimo population after another. Newly imported goods of European manufacture, a shift from hunting for food to hunting for furs to sell, and the introduction of new ideas and beliefs combined to produce profound changes in the Eskimo way of life.

Gradually Eskimos began to spend part of each year near trading posts and missions. Particularly after the fur market collapsed during the Great Depression of the 1930s, the amount of time they spent in these settlements began to increase. In due course schools were built, and considerable pressure began to be placed on Eskimo parents to have their children attend them for several months a year. In the end, they abandoned their migratory way of life and moved into these settlements permanently. The precise sequence of events and the speed with which they occurred varied from one region to another, but by 1970 the members of all Eskimo groups had been absorbed into the modern nation states within whose domain they happened to be residing.

In 1980 about 1300 Eskimos and Aleuts lived in the Soviet Union while 33,000 were in Alaska; Canada and Greenland had Inuit Eskimo populations of about 24,000 and 43,000 respectively. Although many continued to hunt and fish for much of their food, most were also employed, at least seasonally, in the wage economies of their respective countries. Eskimo children went to school, where they learned to speak Russian, English, French (in Quebec) or Danish (in Greenland), and where they were introduced to the knowledge and values of the West. Electricity had arrived in most villages, to be followed less than a decade later by television. Dog teams had been replaced by snowmobiles, all-terrain vehicles and aircraft, and skin-covered boats had yielded to wooden and fibreglass motorboats. The traditional Eskimo way of life, after more than 4000 years of vigorous development, had vanished forever from the face of the earth.

Top: As one approaches the barrens west of Hudson Bay from the south, the trees grow progressively shorter and eventually disappear altogether. North of the tree line only shrubs exist to provide shelter for ptarmigan – white, quail-like birds that were an important source of food for many Eskimo groups.

Above: The inhabitants of the forested areas of southcentral and southwestern Alaska were expert workers in wood, as exemplified by this bowl from Kodiak Island. Carved in the shape of a bird, it is decorated with inlaid white seeds and red paint.

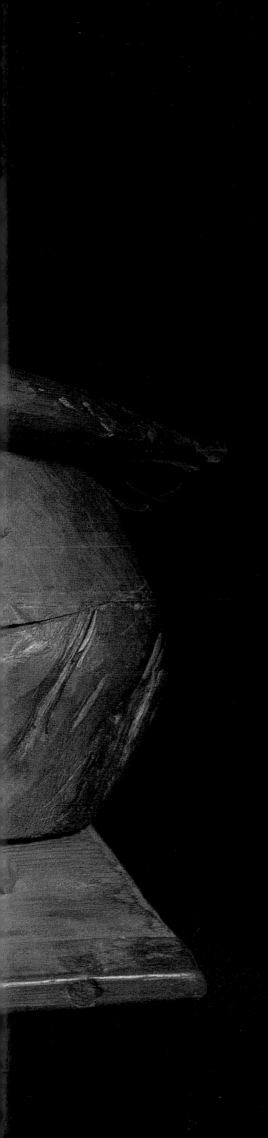

SOCIAL LIFE

Eskimos lived in small, isolated villages. A few may have held as many as 800 inhabitants, but the overwhelming majority were aggregations of only ten to fifty people. The number of dwellings housing that number would vary from one to perhaps six, depending on the region. But even the largest Eskimo settlement that ever existed, separated from its neighbours by many kilometres of unoccupied land, was a mere speck in the vast expanse of the north.

The small, self-contained social world of the Eskimos consisted primarily of relatives. Although their social life was relatively simple, their family life was very complex. A settlement of, say, fifty people, could be occupied by the members of a single family. As a settlement such a group is minute, but as a family it is very large indeed. Among the Western Eskimos, especially the Aleuts, families were sometimes even larger than that.

An Eskimo family could consist solely of a conjugal unit; that is, a husband, wife and their children. Most women had only two or three children despite the fact that Eskimo couples wanted to have as many children as they possibly could. Many investigators have considered the low apparent reproductive rate to be *prima facie* evidence of a high rate of infanticide (see below), which was known to occur in some Eskimo groups. But there is no evidence whatsoever to support that view outside of those specific groups. It is much more likely that the small number of children per woman was the result of two entirely different factors.

One was a high rate of infant mortality – children were born but failed to survive the first year or two. However, there is little in the way of hard evidence to support this assumption either, as far as pre-contact times are concerned.

The second factor, and the more plausible one, is that effective fertility was very low. It could have been low for three reasons. The first was a low ovulation rate due to prolonged breast feeding. Among most Eskimo groups, children were not weaned until they were five or six years old, or even older. Another cause of infrequent, or at least irregular, ovulation might have been extreme leanness, at least seasonally, which is known to lead to amenorrhea among many female athletes today. A final possibility is that many Eskimo women experienced a relatively high rate of spontaneous abortion. This might have occurred during the first few hours or days of pregnancy during periods of extreme physical exertion, such as those involved in travel and in retrieving and butchering the carcasses of large game animals.

This woodcarving represents a shaman in the middle of a seance, and his two helping spirits in the form of animal-like creatures. The shaman is seated on the floor, with his hands tied behind his back; he is leaning forward to touch a sealskin screen suspended between two poles. A drum, which was commonly used to conjure spirits, lies beside him.

Above: Frieda Anniviaq Goodwin (b. 1886), from Northwest Alaska, listened to her parents and grandparents talk about life in the old days when she was a girl. When she reached old age herself, she passed on what she had learned to members of younger generations. This time the information was recorded on paper and tape as a permanent record of a vanished way of life.

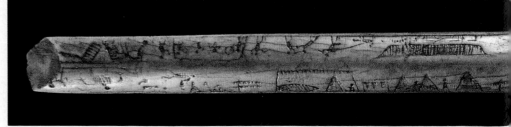

20

We will never know the real answer. We do know, however, that in the twentieth century, after Eskimos became relatively sedentary, and after they started weaning their children at a much earlier age, the birth rate quickly exploded to some of the highest levels ever recorded in any human population.

Most Eskimo families were of the 'extended' variety. That is, they consisted of an array of adult siblings and cousins and their spouses, perhaps one or more aged parents, and children. The mixture was rendered still more complex by the fact that some of the men might have two or three wives, or, in some regions, a few women might have two husbands. In addition to the several kinds of 'blood' relationships, an extended family would also include several varieties of 'in-laws' as well. The typical Eskimo family thus involved a smaller proportion of youngsters, and a much greater number and variety of relatives, than the family which has become institutionalized in the West.

The many relatives and in-laws living together in a settlement often acted as though they were members of a single conjugal family as Westerners would understand it. Cousins, for example, often addressed one another as 'brother' or 'sister', and aunts and uncles treated their nieces and nephews as their children.

Older family members were valued for their wisdom, their knowledge of the customs and taboos of their people, and their ability as storytellers. They were ordinarily cared for with affection, consideration and respect as they attained their senior years. Children, too, were valued – as a form of old-age insurance for their parents, as the only means of perpetuating the society, and, more simply, for their company. The very old and the very young were thought to enhance the quality of family life.

Given the importance that Eskimos attached to the aged, it is surprising that so many Westerners believe that they systematically eliminated elderly people as soon as they became incapable of performing the duties related to hunting or sewing. It is true that, in some regions, when a famine was in progress, an aged person might voluntarily venture out into a storm or into bitter cold weather to starve or freeze to death in order to leave what food there was for younger family members. Or sometimes, when people were moving to new hunting grounds, a heavy load, poor travelling conditions or infirmity might contribute to an elderly person's decision to be left behind without food or shelter. But Eskimos believed that death was just a temporary phase of life, a recycling of the soul from one body to another which would appear in due course. When, during a period of great hunger, an old woman quietly went out to meet certain death in the midst of a raging storm, everyone understood that her soul would return soon in the form of a baby. When a child was born, her name would be bestowed upon it, and within weeks people would notice how this and that trait of the old woman were beginning to emerge in its form and movements.

Infanticide, or the systematic execution of babies, is similarly misunderstood. It was indeed practised in a few Eskimo groups from time to time. It was most common in regions where life was particularly harsh, but even there it normally occurred only during an extreme shortage of food. However, with, rare exceptions, infants were put to death – usually by freezing – only before they had been given a name. In the Eskimo view, a body without a name was not yet a human being; it was just a thing. So putting a nameless infant out in the snow was not

Women carried babies and young children in the backs, not the hoods, of their parkas. The warmth and the physical contact with the mother combined to impart a profound sense of well-being to the child, whether asleep or awake. This wood carving depicts an East Greenland woman with the characteristic (but slightly exaggerated) hairdo of the region, wearing a lightweight parka and short summer trousers made from sealskin. Her baby observes the scene over her shoulder.

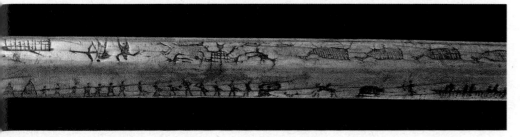

Left: Handles made of bone or ivory were favourite places for people to record events and views of daily life. This broken ivory bow-drill handle contains incised sketches of hunting and travel scenes.

murder. But whether a child had been named or not, infanticide was a desperate measure resorted to only in times of duress.

Eskimos generally liked to be surrounded by as many kin as possible. Indeed, a family of hundreds or even thousands of people was the ultimate goal of Eskimo family development. This ideal was never even remotely approached in reality because strains within the family and lack of food prevented it.

The personal relations among the members of an Eskimo family were incredibly intense, since the same few people might spend most of their time together for months or even years on end. People knew each other so well that the slightest gesture or facial expression could serve to communicate a complex idea or sentiment. If food was abundant, if the family was wisely managed by its leaders, and if everyone's personality meshed perfectly with everyone else's, then a family could be a harmonious social unit. But if food was scarce, as it occasionally was; if the family leaders acted imprudently, as they sometimes did; or if two or more personalities clashed, as they eventually were bound to — family relationships could become a burden.

Relief from pent-up tension was provided by moves of the entire family from one hunting ground to another, by visits to or from other families, by games and other recreational activities, and by festivals and feasts. But a permanent solution

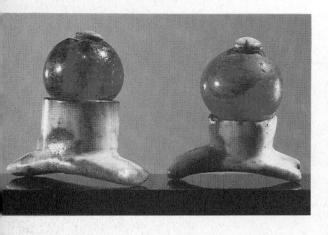

Above: In Northwest Alaska men's fashion decreed the use of labrets — ivory, stone or wooden plugs inserted through holes cut in the lower lip, usually one on each side of the mouth. The cuts were made during the teenage years, but there apparently was no formal rite de passage involved. This pair, with valuable blue trade beads affixed to the end of each one, probably belonged to a wealthy man.

Right: This leather bracelet displays four small ivory figurines representing stylized animals. Carvings similar to these were common, and served variously as decoration, charms, toys and game pieces.

could be achieved only through a division of the family unit. A disaffected couple might set out for a time on its own, but this would be risky because all the best hunting grounds would be already occupied. The couple would be more likely to join another group of relatives living some distance away from the first. Alternatively, two or three conjugal families might break off as a group to form a new settlement of their own. This division process helped keep the size of extended families far below the ideal maximum, but it also served to reduce tension. However, it really was just a matter of leaving one extended family and joining another, not of avoiding family life altogether. The only alternative was total isolation, which meant certain death, given the realities of northern life.

The fact that Eskimo families often did achieve reasonably stable sizes of two or three dozen people with some regularity may be attributed to a combination of generally good leadership and their hierarchical power structure. Parents had authority over their children, and senior family members generally had authority over junior ones (although old people acted more as advisers than as leaders). This pattern was interrupted only by the authority of males over females in several spheres of decision making, such as when and where to move camp.

The hierarchical structure of Eskimo families has been consistently overlooked by Westerners, partly because of their inability to understand the language, and

Long-visored bentwood headgear was worn by Aleut men early in the nineteenth century to indicate their status and nationality. They were made by skilled craftsmen from a single piece of wood with the two ends joined at the back, and fastened together with sinew. Realistic or stylized ivory carvings and amulets, sea lion bristles, and glass and ivory beads completed the decoration, much of which was apparently of magical as well as aesthetic value.

partly because it never occurred to them to look for a hierarchy at the family level; but mostly they missed it because of the quiet way in which Eskimos exercised authority. A family head would say in a normal voice, as part of a general conversation, 'We are getting low on seal meat.' A Western observer would regard that merely as a statement of fact. The man's son, however, would understand it as an instruction to go seal hunting. A man on a hunting expedition with his two sons might say 'I'm thirsty'. The older son would glance briefly at the younger one, who would know that he had just been given an order to fetch some water for his father. If three sons were along instead of two, there would be a second glance, and the youngest – the one at the bottom of the hierarchy – would go and get the water. Despite the subtlety with which it was manifested, the authority structure of an extended family was very well defined.

Outside the family, most Eskimo societies were egalitarian in the sense that they did not distinguish offices which set one person above another on a society-wide basis, although the Aleuts and Pacific Eskimos did have hereditary village chiefs. However, Eskimos recognized and respected superior intelligence and ability, and the sphere of influence of a truly exceptional person sometimes extended over an entire society even though his span of control technically did not go beyond the limits of his own family.

Capable family heads attracted large followings of relatives. The greater their ability, the larger their group of adherents became. Effective leadership required not only personal charisma and demonstrated success as a hunter, but a sensibility to and understanding of human relations. The successful family head watched closely for signs of conflict or tension, and attempted to prevent or mediate any that might arise. One who failed in these aspects of his duties would be abandoned by his relatives just as promptly as one who made a series of bad decisions about where to look for game.

Even the most effectively managed family could not remain large for a prolonged period of time because of limits on the food supply. Except in some parts of the Aleutian Islands and Southwest Alaska, lean seasons repeatedly forced groups of more than fifty people to divide into segments. The segments, each of which was a smaller and less complex version of the original family unit, spread out across the country seeking supplies of fish and game to tide them over until better times. In most regions, periods of scarcity were so regular in their occurrence that people anticipated them in their annual cycle of movement. Rather than waiting for a famine to strike, then attempting to move when already weakened by hunger, large families divided and dispersed before the lean season even began. When conditions improved, or when they reliably could be expected to improve, the various groups re-united.

Within each family, no matter what its size, there was a strict division of

This incised bow drill handle segment illustrates a number of scenes. On the lower right is a summer camp of conical skin tents and several people, most of whom appear to be playing a game. A grazing caribou is seen on the lower left. Just above those scenes, but viewed from the top, is a hunter spearing swimming caribou from a kayak. He has already killed three, and is pursuing four others. He will probably take the hindmost with several quick thrusts to the kidneys, but the three in front seem about to escape. The final scene, just above the ridge on the handle, is unclear. The end of the handle, on the left, is carved in the shape of an antlerless caribou head (viewed here from the top).

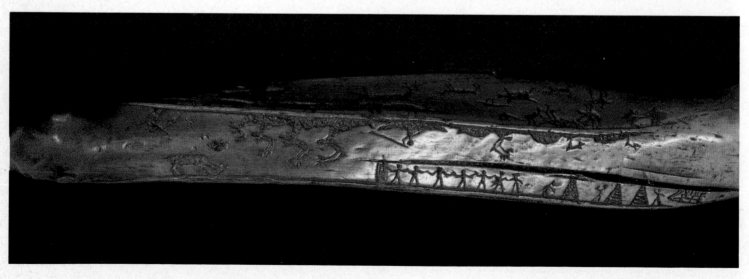

24

labour between males and females. Men were responsible for all big game hunting; for the construction of houses and boats; for the manufacture of tools, weapons, utensils and appurtenances made of wood, stone, bone and ivory; and for the protection of the family from physical danger. Women were responsible for the processing of all game and the preparation of food; for all work in skins and grass; for the gathering of most vegetable products, such as leaves, berries, grass and roots; and for the general operation of the household. The pursuit of small game and certain varieties of birds and fish either was shared, or differed between men's and women's work from one region to another.

In some regions the members of even very large extended families lived in communal houses. Each conjugal family had a separate sleeping area within the house, partially screened off from the others. This was so in parts of Greenland, in Labrador, and in at least the eastern Aleutian Islands, where an entire settlement could consist of a single household.

Elsewhere, houses were too small to contain so many people, but the same

Winter houses in Southwest Alaska were dug a metre or more (three or four feet) into the ground, lined with timber and covered with sod. They were impervious to cold and wind, but too warm and damp for summer use. Here we see part of a reconstructed house near Becharof Lake, on the Alaska Peninsula, which had two dwelling levels, one just below the ground's surface, and a second that was fully subterranean.

25

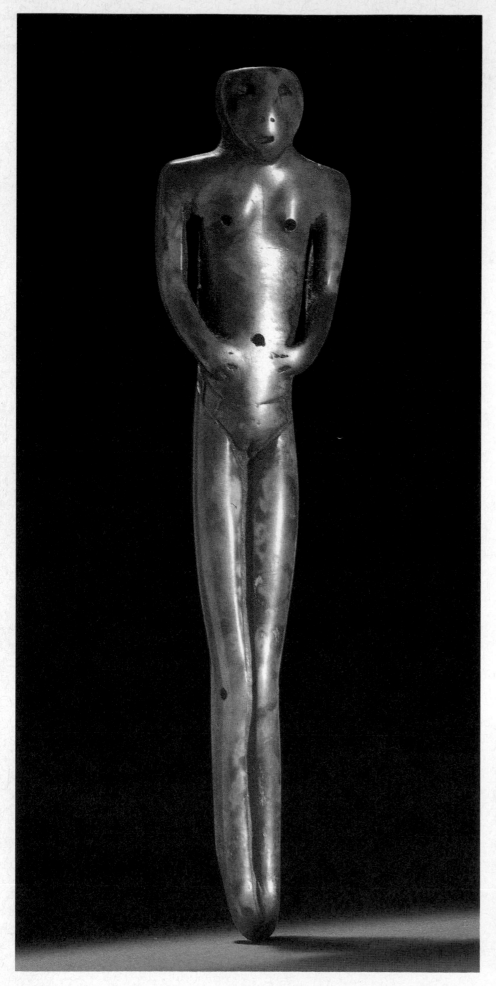

Left: Since women had to make and repair all of their family's clothing, a ready supply of needles was a necessity. To prevent loss, needles were stored in special cases, which were carved into an incredible array of shapes, such as this female figure. This is not a doll, but a hollow tube full of needles.

Below: Women used an ulu, *a knife made of a bevelled slate (or metal) blade and a bone, ivory or wood handle. Manipulated by dexterous wrist movements, it was used in butchering meat, removing blubber from skins, sewing – virtually all of the many tasks women performed where knives were needed.*

basic principle of residential proximity still applied. When a family was too large to fit into one house, its members built two or three. They were close together and often linked by tunnels or passageways, and the occupants of all of them remained under the supervision of a single family head. Children moved freely from one house to another, the women congregated in one to pass the time of day as they sewed or mended clothes, and the men worked together in another when they were not out hunting. All ate together; or, if there were too many people to fit into one house, the men and older boys ate in one dwelling, and the women, girls and young children took their meals in another. Children often slept in whatever house they happened to be in when they got tired.

In parts of Alaska many families were so large that ordinary dwellings no longer sufficed for the gatherings of even the men. When that occurred they erected a separate building, known as a 'kashim', to serve as the men's daily work, eating and gathering place. Women and children spent their day in smaller groups in two or three of the dwellings in the family cluster, but on ceremonial or festive occasions, all were welcome in the 'kashim'. In the Central Arctic, the 'kashim' was usually a large snow house erected between (and sometimes literally on top of) dwelling units, and was occupied by women and playing children as much as by men.

In parts of the Western Arctic where food was particularly abundant, a settlement might be inhabited by two or more large extended families. In some of the whaling villages on the Northwest Alaskan coast, for example, six or seven might be located in one vicinity, perhaps near the end of a prominent point of land. A settlement of this type is best understood as being several different villages which happened to be located very close together, not as a single cohesive unit. Each family erected its houses in a discrete cluster, each had its own 'kashim', and each operated pretty much independently of all the others.

Eskimo families were generally autonomous. In most regions geographic isolation made family independence a necessity, but self-sufficiency in practically every area of life was what made it possible. Family members could produce all the goods and services required for their own survival, they could control or mediate most of the disruptive tendencies of their members, and they could attend to their own religious and recreational needs. Family autonomy enabled Eskimos to respond to famine or other disasters by splitting up and dispersing over the countryside, thus dividing the risk of failure among several different parts of the population. The segmental nature of Eskimo societies was one of the keys to survival in the harsh northern setting.

No family was *completely* independent of all the others. As a minimum, different families depended on one another to provide spouses for members of the younger generation. In very small populations the location of a suitable spouse is

Side-bladed knives, with bone handles and bevelled, chipped-stone or metal blades, served as men's whittling tools. Stone tools were used in the north until recent times, but some metal is thought to have penetrated the Eskimo area through trade as much as a thousand years ago.

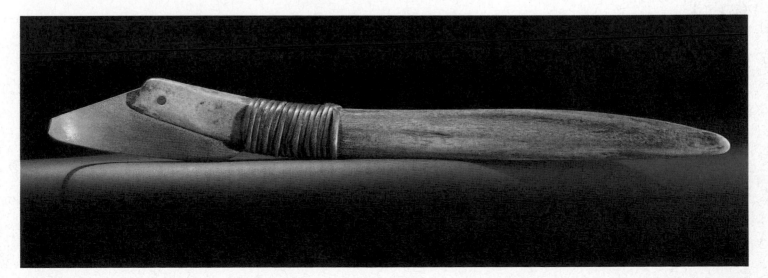

often a difficult matter because there are not enough people of the appropriate age and sex to go round. In addition to personal considerations, such as physical attractiveness, hunting or sewing ability and personality, Eskimos had to consider incest problems. For example, if one was forbidden to marry a cousin, but if the only potential spouses in the entire society were cousins, one was faced with a crisis. In regions where the population was both small and widely dispersed, such as the Central Arctic and parts of Greenland, young people often gave up and married a cousin anyway, despite disapproval from the rest of the community. The Caribou Eskimos, who had one of the most scattered populations ever recorded, turned the whole thing around and actually encouraged the marriage of cousins.

Eskimo marriage took several different forms. The most fundamental involved a man and woman taking up residence together and having sexual relations. There was no ceremony, gift exchange or other sign of formal recognition at the start of such a marriage. In most regions the two simply set up housekeeping on their own; or, more often, one spouse moved in with the other's family and became part of that household. The Aleuts and some Southwest Alaskan groups practised 'bride service': a suitor lived with and worked for a girl's family for several months or more. If he proved acceptable, the two would be permitted to sleep together. Some time later, they would join the household of the husband's parents or other relatives.

The manner in which spouses were selected varied from one region to another. The most common practice was similar to that in the West: a man and woman fell in love and decided to marry. Parents and other relatives tried to influence the selection, but in most areas they had little effective control over it. In some regions, however, there was a system of formal betrothal. Among the Caribou Eskimos parents arranged their children's marriages, often while the principals were still infants. Eventually, the betrothed youngsters would be pressured into taking up joint residence, and sexual relations would follow in due course.

There were two other forms of residential marriage, both of them polygamous. The more common was the polygynous union of one man and two women. This type of arrangement was the prerogative of the rich and powerful, for only an exceptional hunter could feed two wives and their offspring as well as an aged parent or two. An outstanding hunter actually needed two wives, since one alone could not process all the game he would produce.

The second wife would be taken after the original couple had been together for some time. The first was supposed to be the dominant one, both in the husband's sentiments and in the practical management of the household. Occasionally, especially when the second wife was much younger than the first, the tendency for the husband to prefer her for lovemaking complicated the situation. It was even more complicated if more than two wives were involved, but that did not happen very often or in very many societies.

The second form of polygamous marriage was the polyandrous residential union of two men and one woman. Such arrangements were rare in the Eskimo world generally, although in regions where women were in short supply, and among the Aleuts, they did exist. Polyandrous unions seem to have been subject to more stress than polygynous ones were. This was not only because of sexual rivalry between the two husbands, but also because of the burden that would be imposed on a woman having to process the game produced by two hunters.

The three forms of residential marriage constituted only part of the Eskimo marriage system. There also was a *non*-residential form of marriage. This practice is widely referred to in the West as 'wife exchange' or 'wife trading', but is more accurately and dispassionately characterized as 'co-marriage'. A co-marriage came into existence when two couples temporarily exchanged sexual partners. Sometimes wives were coerced into these unions; usually, they were not.

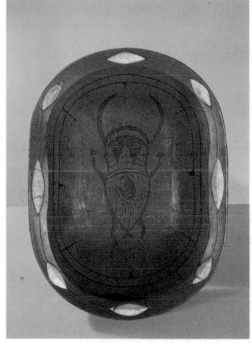

Above: In Alaska men and older boys spent much of their time working or visiting in a separate building, the 'kashim'. In some regions they also slept there. The women brought food to them in trays or bowls, of which this is an elegant example. It has been dyed red and painted with a figure of some grotesque mythological creature. The bentwood rim is decorated with pieces of white stone.

Left: This parka from the central Canadian Arctic displays the characteristic small front flap and long back flap that symbolized the female sex over most of the Eskimo area. It is made of several caribou skins cut and pieced together to form an attractive garment. The leather belt, fastened with wooden toggles, kept the baby on the woman's back from falling out.

Co-marriage was a form of *marriage*, not the expression of primitive lust it is often represented to have been. The union was regarded as permanent even if the sexual act which established it was never repeated, and it involved the participants in an enduring set of mutual obligations of sharing, protection and support. It also made siblings of all of the offspring that were ever born to any of the participants, which made cousins of the descendants in the third generation.

A traditional Eskimo society may be conceived of as being made up of a group of relatively independent extended families related to each other by marriage. Over the generations the ties of marriage of course yielded ties of blood, connecting the members of different families through additional kinship ties.

These 'natural' interfamily links were augmented by the widespread practice of adoption. Almost every Eskimo family of more than a dozen people contained at least one youngster who had been adopted into it. Conversely, almost every such family gave away one of its youngsters in adoption to another family. These arrangements always occurred between families whose members were already very good friends, or, more often, already related in some way. In contrast to the custom in the West, an adopted child would regard both the biological and the adopting couples as his parents; the arrangement would strengthen the ties between two families instead of replacing one set of parents with another. Among many of the societies in the Yupik language area, still more interfamily links were provided by lineages and clans.

Namesake relationships formed one of the few social mechanisms connecting the members of separate families that was not based entirely on kinship ties. The mystical power attributed to names perhaps made it inevitable that *any* people who had the same name would regard themselves as being linked in a special way, whether they were related or not. In some regions namesakes gave each other presents from time to time, while in others they participated jointly in dances or festivals. But in all groups except the Asiatic Eskimos, the namesake tie served as an important strand in the web which bound the members of different families into a larger social system.

Finally, there were 'partnerships'. A partnership was a voluntary relationship entered into by two people not otherwise related. The form it took varied from one region to another. In some places partnership was expressed by the two people dancing together on certain occasions. In others, partners engaged in the ritual sharing of seal flippers. A third pattern required elaborate, ritualized joking. The common theme of partnerships was sharing and gift giving.

The generosity with which all of these relationships were imbued represented one of the most fundamental social values of the Eskimos: sharing. Other equally important values were courtesy, emotional control, forbearance, peacefulness, honesty, obedience to elders, fidelity to kin, and faithful adherence to taboos. Only the last was reinforced by supernatural authority. The Eskimos distinguished between right and wrong, but they lacked the concept of 'sin' as a general offence against God or religious law. What was right or wrong was determined by custom, but custom is a very powerful force among small, isolated groups with little or no exposure to alien ideas.

Conformity to tradition was not enforced by organizations external to the family. There were no legislatures to establish laws, no courts to interpret them or to adjudicate disputes, no governments to manage societal affairs, and no legally constituted means of coercion available to curb disruptive behaviour.

The Eskimos did have ways to discourage troublemaking, however. The most common way was ridicule, which often emerged subtly in the context of teasing or idle play. If a young man had been taking a disproportionate amount of food, the others' displeasure might be brought to his attention in an impromptu song about the negative attributes of greedy people. Among Western Eskimos, if this did not solve the problem, family elders might advise or even command the person to stop eating so much. Among Eastern Eskimos, such overt wielding of

Above: The traditional East Greenland tupilaq was a grotesque figurine carved of ivory, bone or wood. It was created and animated by a shaman for the purpose of bringing harm to someone else. Nowadays such figurines are still made, but for sale to tourists and art collectors. They are one of the few traditional forms to survive into modern times.

Facing page: In many regions disputes were settled through dances and song contests in which opponents ridiculed each other in front of other members of the community. The custom was especially well developed in East Greenland, where this mask originated. It was worn by one of the disputants during such a dance.

31

authority was generally considered improper. They would make the same point in a different way – through elaborate ridicule in the form of lampoon songs. In some regions they even had lampoon contests between disaffected parties. The people involved sang songs of derision right in one another's face while standing before the assembled community. Public opinion, as gauged by audience response, ordinarily settled the matter.

The most extreme non-physical means of dealing with a troublemaker was to shun him (or her), literally to pretend the person did not exist. No one would talk to him, no one would give anything to him or take anything from him; and if possible, camp would be moved without that person's knowledge. Given the Eskimos' gregarious nature, shunning was a devastating rebuke.

Ridicule and shunning were inadequate when physical violence occurred, however, as it did from time to time. A classic Eskimo example would be a man deciding he wanted someone else's wife, and determining to take her by force, if necessary, despite the weight of negative public opinion. The result depended on pragmatic considerations. If the husband was a powerful man, and especially if he had the support of several brothers and male cousins, the suitor would be physically prevented from carrying out his intentions; if the positions of strength and weakness were reversed, the suitor would be likely to achieve his goal. If he did, even though his actions were contrary to Eskimo standards of behaviour, he would not have to be concerned about either incarceration by police or condemnation to Hell by an outraged God. For the rest of his life, however, he would have to be alert to the possibility of assassination by the humiliated husband.

Assassination was the ultimate check against disruptive behaviour. In the most extreme cases, members of a troublemaker's own family proceeded collectively to take this action. When that happened, the death of the offender ended the affair. In less extreme cases, which meant most of the time, only a single individual, or perhaps a group of brothers, carried out an assassination. Far from ending the trouble, this served to expand and perpetuate it because of the powerful Eskimo ethic of fidelity to kin.

Killing, no matter how justified in some cases, set in motion a blood feud. The closest male relative of a murdered person was obliged to seek vengeance by assassinating the killer. Revenge was not necessarily sought immediately, however. Often it was postponed for years while the people involved played a game of cat and mouse. In public they acted as though nothing was wrong, while privately the avenger sought a favourable opportunity to eliminate the murderer. Sometimes a murderer would undertake pre-emptive action, but that compounded his crime, and merely transferred the obligation of vengeance to someone else.

In theory there was no end to the feuding process: one murder led inevitably to another in a perpetual cycle of retribution. In practice this rarely occurred. Often a murderer and the one most responsible for seeking vengeance were close relatives, which placed the latter in a quandary. Also, the obligation to avenge

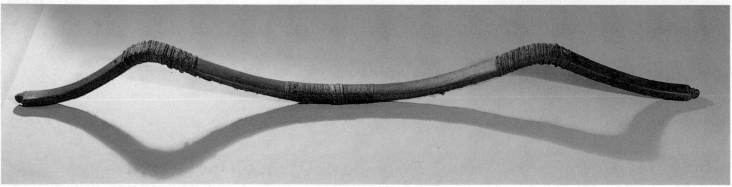

Above: This model umiak shows the primary western Alaskan mode of summer travel. Seen here are the helmsman, usually an elderly man, and members of his family manning the oars. All are dressed in waterproof seal intestine parkas.

Left: A primary weapon for both hunting and fighting was the bow, which was produced in a variety of shapes across the Arctic. This example from the Central Arctic shows the recurved shape characteristic of bows made in that region. The sinew backing added strength and resilience.

was offset by a number of other values, such as emotional control and a belief in non-violence. If the initial murder seemed justified, and if enough time elapsed without incident for tempers to cool, a feud might not develop. Alternatively, the murderer might flee the country. Such an act was fraught with risk, but it still might be safer than staying at home. The theoretical potential for anarchy in Eskimo societies is not known ever to have been realized in fact.

Eskimo social structures may not have been well designed to control disruptive behaviour, but they were very good at promoting the maintenance of harmonious relations. Eskimo settlements were isolated, but Eskimo individuals were not. They were surrounded by people all the time, and most of them were supportive. Individual privacy, in the Western sense, did not exist, nor, indeed, was it considered desirable. People worked, played, ate, slept and loafed in groups; in some areas they made love in groups as well. Relatives and partners who had to live apart because of the dispersed nature of their food resources visited each other as often as they could.

The number of families who would be linked together in a network of social relations was not very large. An Eskimo's social world, at its widest, consisted of perhaps fifteen to forty extended families related to each other socially and geographically, but separated in both respects from all other groups. Within each network people were connected through ties of kinship, name and partnership. They spoke a distinctive dialect or sub-dialect, wore a distinctive style of clothing, and shared customs and traditions which differed in detail from those of all other Eskimo groups despite the common cultural heritage. The members of each network also owned in common a specific territory.

The discrete social and territorial networks which comprised the Eskimo world have been variously referred to as 'tribes' and 'societies'. Whatever the label, they were the Eskimo counterpart of modern nations. They all manifested variations of a single general cultural tradition, but each was a separate political and territorial unit. Eskimo societies were analogous in these respects to England, Canada, New Zealand, Australia and the United States. Life in all five countries is dominated by English cultural tradition, but each is nonetheless a separate political and territorial entity.

Just how many Eskimo societies there were at any given point in time is not known. A preliminary estimate for the first quarter of the nineteenth century suggests a minimum figure of 140 for the Eskimo area as a whole. The true number was probably closer to 200.

In the early nineteenth century, Eskimo societies appear to have involved about 450 people, on average, with about 150 and 2000 being the extreme limits. Territorially, they were much more impressive. In parts of Southwest Alaska, the Aleutian Islands and Asia societal territories might be as small as 1000 square kilometres (395 square miles), but in the Central and Eastern Arctic some encompassed areas exceeding 200,000 square kilometres (77,220 square miles). In one or two cases population density was as low as one person per 400 square kilometres (150 square miles) of societal territory.

The citizens of most of these societies knew each other. In the very smallest, they were all related by blood, marriage, or both. In such cases a woman could simply glance at a piece of clothing and know who had made it, and a man could briefly examine a piece of chipped stone or a length of sealskin rope and identify its maker.

The citizens of each society were similarly knowledgeable about their own country. From infancy on, they travelled back and forth across it, stopping here for a week, there for a month, constantly studying the terrain for what it could tell them about the presence or absence of game, the location of material for stone tools, or the availability of sod for housing material. But the world outside was poorly known. Among the Polar Eskimos of Northwest Greenland this ignorance was absolute. Completely cut off by ice and barren waste from all other human populations, they thought they were the only people in the entire world when they were encountered by Sir John Ross in 1818. Among the Western Eskimos, on the other hand, where patterns of inter-societal contact and travel were highly developed, knowledge of neighbouring peoples and lands was reasonably accurate and complete.

Relations between societies ranged from non-existent, in the case of the Polar

Tobacco was carried by an international trade network from America across Europe and Siberia to Alaska in the mid-eighteenth century. When Europeans arrived shortly thereafter, the Eskimos were already addicted to it. This elegantly carved and decorated ivory pipe carries its own cleaner in rings attached to the top.

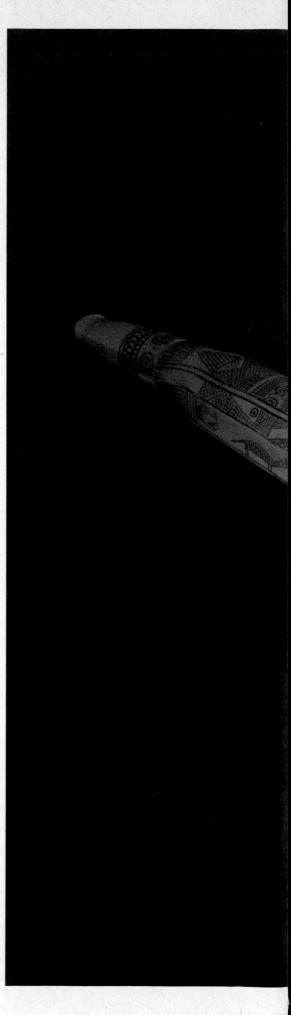

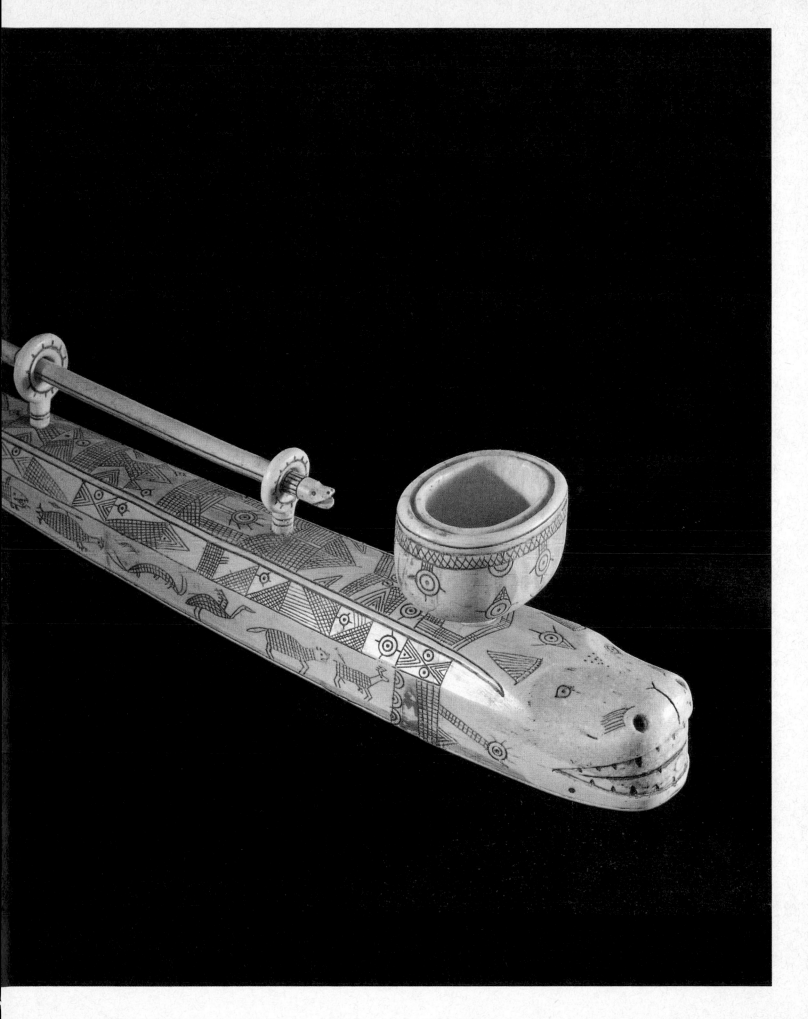

Eskimos, to structured and complex, in Alaska. In all areas the members of other societies were regarded with prejudice and mistrust, often with outright fear. Members of neighbouring societies were regarded as inferior to the members of one's own. They were lazy, stupid, impotent, incompetent and dishonest; they spoke a bizarre dialect, and exhibited strange behaviour. Members of more distant societies, often known only through rumour or legend, typically were imbued with more sinister, often inhuman, characteristics.

The land between many societal territories in the Central and Eastern Arctic was often all but uninhabitable. In such cases there was little or no contact between the members of neighbouring societies. When it did occur, by accident, it usually involved only a small family group on each side. Lacking any traditional guidelines on how they should act under such circumstances, the people often fled. Occasionally one group – particularly if it was much larger – might attack the other. Sometimes, however, these chance encounters were peaceful,

Women used sealskin thimbles when sewing. They were easily lost amid the household clutter or during travel, so for safe keeping they were placed on thimble guards when not in use. These, in turn, were attached to needle cases. The thimble guard shown here represents some kind of creature carrying a seal on its back.

the people involved being too curious to flee, too frightened to fight, and ignorant of any way of dealing with people other than that of ordinary polite discourse. Meetings of this sort sometimes led to the establishment of lasting personal ties between the members of the two parties.

Trade provided the one enduring opportunity for peaceful inter-societal contact in most parts of the Eskimo world. The territory of every society contained some commodity – a type of rock, a species of animal, a supply of wood – either in greater supply, or of better quality, than any of its neighbours. In addition, some individuals were particularly skilled – in sewing waterproof boots, perhaps, or in constructing powerful bows. Both raw materials and manufactured products served as bases of inter-societal trade because of these differences. In a few regions inter-societal trade was conducted on a strictly *ad hoc* basis, whenever a chance meeting occurred. In many others, it took place more regularly when a few families got together by pre-arrangement. In parts of Alaska and Greenland, however, inter-societal trade was carried out so regularly and on such a large scale that what amounted to international trade fairs, involving hundreds and even thousands of people, were held in certain locations during each summer.

No matter how many might be gathered at one place, each person knew who was a fellow citizen and who was not. In Alaska, where the boundaries of societal territories were precisely defined, it was equally clear whether or not one was in home territory. People periodically entered an alien country without invitation, or in a manner not in keeping with certain long-standing customs, but when

they did, they were presumed to be on a hostile errand and were treated accordingly. Borders ordinarily were crossed only by groups accepting invitations, by groups travelling according to previously established custom, or by raiding parties. In contrast to the Eastern Eskimos, who engaged in very little systematic inter-societal violence, Western Eskimos frequently engaged in raiding and sometimes in full-scale war.

Raids usually were undertaken to redress an insult or to avenge a killing. In Northwest Alaska these seem to have been the only reasons for which war was waged, and the sole tactical objective was to kill people. The Aleuts and Pacific Eskimos also raided for the purpose of taking captives, whom they pressed into slavery. In a few regions an additional objective was to recover booty. Nowhere in the Eskimo world was raiding or warfare known to have been undertaken for the purpose of acquiring new territory.

The favourite Western Eskimo strategy was the night-time raid. The most desired tactic was to catch the entire population of the target settlement involved in some sort of festivity in the 'kashim', oblivious to danger. The raiders barred the door, then threw firebrands or smoking debris in through the skylight. The occupants burned to death or suffocated; any who attempted to escape were killed as they emerged from the building. Achieving this straightforward objective was seldom easy, however. Often the inhabitants of target villages were forewarned by friends or relatives living in the other society, by hunters who had seen the approaching raiders, or, at the last moment, by howling dogs. In such

Among the Western Eskimos open battle usually began with a firefight. Drawn up in battle lines about 150–200 metres (150–200 yards) apart, the opposing sides attempted to reduce the enemy force by well-directed arrows. At extreme range they often could be dodged, but extra protection for the vital organs was provided by plate armour made of strips of bone or ivory lashed together into a vest-like arrangement that was held up by shoulder straps.

Asiatic Eskimos, who were often at war with one another or with neighbouring Chukchi, supplemented plate armour with a cuirass. This example from St Lawrence Island, viewed from the front, is made from pieces of wood covered by de-haired sealskins. It was held up with chest and arm straps.

cases they ambushed the raiders as they approached the village, or sent out a force to confront them well beyond its borders. Often, only some of the people would be in the 'kashim', and the others could come to their assistance. Western Eskimo men were almost always armed, so they could begin to mount a defence at the very first cry of alarm. Additional measures included building settlements in places that were difficult to approach, placing rows of bone or baleen (whale-bone) spikes around the village so as to pierce the boots of unsuspecting night raiders, and building 'kashims' and houses with secret escape tunnels.

Most raids involved only a dozen or so men on a side. Occasionally, however, there were armed confrontations in which the combatants numbered in the hundreds. Alaskan Eskimos had some knowledge of how to form and manoeuvre battle lines. They engaged in both fire tactics (armed with bows and arrows) and shock tactics (armed with clubs, spears and knives). They often wore protective clothing in the form of special fur or skin vests, and in some regions they wore plate armour manufactured from pieces of bone or ivory linked together with rawhide.

The value of non-violence obviously did not apply universally. It was strongest within the extended family, weaker between extended families (which was the sphere within which most blood feuds took place), and it scarcely existed at all between societies. At this third level, the Western stereotype of the peaceful, smiling Eskimo vanishes into thin air, to be replaced by an image of people who were at best fearful and suspicious, and at worst aggressively hostile.

When a human silhouette appeared within view of an Eskimo settlement, its identification was a crucial matter. Most settlements were so small that everyone in them knew who was out hunting and which way they had gone. Armed with this information and with their familiarity with one another, they usually could recognize members of their own settlement while they were still specks in the distance. If they were not promptly identified as local people, a yell of alarm would be given. Everybody would come out to study the approaching figures. Because each society had a characteristic clothing style – a distinctive hood shape or trim arrangement, perhaps – it was usually possible to complete the assessment while the strangers were still hundreds of metres away.

If the approaching strangers were judged to be foreigners, the next question was whether or not they were intent on hostilities. The presence of women and children in the party suggested not. If a mixed group, the women and children of the camp merely stood off to one side; if the strangers were all men, they ran and tried to hide. In either case, the men of the settlement armed themselves and formed a line in front of the village. What happened next depended on the purposes of the arriving party. Sometimes there was bloodshed, while at other times an uneasy truce was established. But it was always a situation fraught with tension.

On the other hand, if, upon distant examination, the approaching strangers were identified as relatives or friends, the reaction was totally different. There would be a great flurry of excited activity as the women readied food, and the men prepared to help the travellers unload their sleds and feed their dogs. Hours of feasting, dancing, storytelling, trading, games and gossip would follow, everyone rejoicing in the fellowship which had broken the solitude of their tiny settlement.

Bentwood tubs had a variety of uses, such as hauling water, holding food or storing urine to be used in processing hides. This one from southwestern Alaska has a painted caribou head on the side.

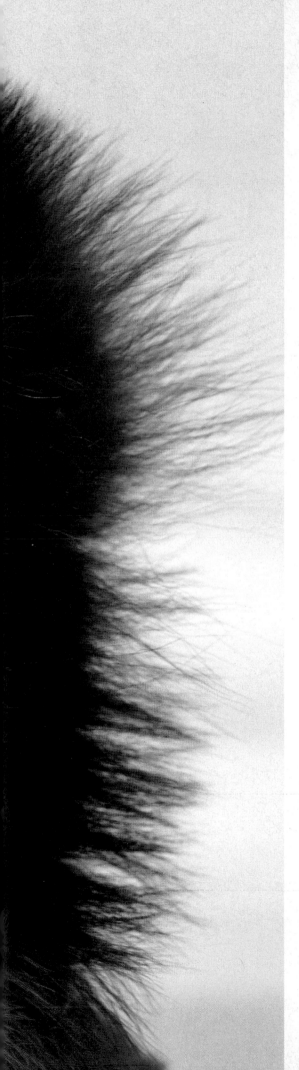

FIGHTING THE
COLD

'Raw', not 'cold', is the word which most accurately characterizes the climate of the Eskimo area as a whole. In the Aleut and the Pacific and Asiatic Eskimo sectors this quality is manifested in the form of persistent strong winds, high relative humidity, and temperatures that seldom deviate much from the freezing point. In many other coastal areas the relative humidity is lower, but so also is the temperature, and the wind is every bit as strong. In interior Alaska it is relatively dry and the winds are not so severe, but winter temperatures are bitterly cold. In most of the Central and Eastern Arctic constant winds and low temperatures are the dominant weather features. But no matter what word is used to describe northern weather, the various elements that comprise it conspire in one way or another to deprive both man and beast of the body heat required to sustain life.

Windchill, rather than cold as such, was the Eskimos' major climatic problem. Windchill is a measure of the combined effect of wind speed and temperature on the loss of body heat; the chill produced by a given temperature is geometrically increased by a rise in wind speed. Combating – or, more accurately, avoiding or reducing – the effects of windchill was an all-pervasive concern.

The first line of defence against the harsh climate was clothing. The simplest clothing was worn by Aleuts and Pacific Eskimos, who had to contend with weather that was rarely cold, but usually windy and wet. Their outfit consisted of a long pullover shirt with a high collar and tight-fitting neck, over which a hooded, waterproof windbreaker, called a *kamleika*, was often worn. Amazingly, Aleuts often went barefoot.

In most other areas clothing consisted of a hooded shirt (or parka), trousers, boots and mittens. The basic wardrobe was generally the same for both men and women, although the cut and trim usually differed according to sex, and in some regions women's trousers and boots were combined in a single garment.

Many early European explorers described Eskimos as being fat. In fact, it was their bulky, loose-fitting clothing which made them appear so. This clothing, so unattractive to European eyes, was probably the most effective cold weather apparel ever devised. Someone wearing a two-layer winter costume made from caribou skins could stay comfortable for a prolonged period of time at a temperature of -50° centigrade (-58° Fahrenheit) in an outfit weighing only about four and a half kilograms (ten pounds).

The greatest problem with Eskimo clothing was that it did not 'breathe'. Transpiration, or the normal 'breathing' of the skin, produces moisture which,

A parka made use of the air trap principle whereby body heat was prevented from escaping. Leonard Putu Vestal (1892–1975), an elder from Kotzebue, Alaska, is seen here wearing a hood with a wolverine fur ruff, which provided protection for his face from wind.

under most conditions, evaporates. In very cold weather, however, this moisture condenses and accumulates on a person's skin and clothing, particularly if the latter is airtight. Eventually it freezes, first on the outer layer, then on the inner one, and finally on the skin. Consequently, Eskimos were always drying their clothes. Before a person entered a house he would brush off the snow and hoarfrost which had accumulated so they would not melt and dampen the clothing in the warm interior. Once inside, the boots and at least the outer clothing layer would be removed, turned inside out, and hung to dry.

Perspiration compounded the problem. It is astonishing how hot one can become from vigorous physical exertion in even the coldest weather, and in extreme cold perspiration condenses and eventually freezes. To keep themselves from becoming overheated, Eskimo hunters moved at a measured pace rather than at a brisk walk, and they tried to release any excess heat trapped inside their clothing by pushing the hood back from their face, loosening the belt, or removing completely the outer layer.

Eskimo winter clothing was so effective in protecting the wearer from the elements that it almost provided clothing and shelter at the same time. Hunters living in the interior of Northwest Alaska used to set forth on a two- or three-day walking trip to search for caribou without taking any shelter with them. Despite the fact that they might be outside in temperatures in the vicinity of -30° centigrade (-22° Fahrenheit) or below for the entire period, all they took with them was weapons, some food (in the form of dried meat or fish and a small bag of seal oil), and an extra pair of boots and insoles in case the ones they were wearing became too damp or were torn. At night, or when they needed a rest, they took a few minutes to make a windbreak out of snow. Each man then removed his gloves and sat on them. Next he withdrew his arms from the sleeves and folded them across his chest. Finally, he leaned forward with his arms against his knees so as not to fall over (if he fell the warm air inside would escape around the bottom of the parka), and fell asleep.

Shelter was the second line of defence against the cold. Unfortunately, weather could never be the sole, or necessarily even the most important, consideration in its construction. The availability of building material was equally

The need for warm clothing is immediately apparent in this photo of an ice-covered West Greenland fiord and the surrounding windswept hills.

important, as was the need for movement. The structure of an Eskimo dwelling was always a compromise between three competing factors: warmth, materials and mobility, and all three varied from one region to another.

The basic Eskimo dwelling was a semi-subterranean sod house. It was 'semi-subterranean' because it was dug into the ground, but only about a metre (just over three feet) or so. It was constructed of a framework of wood or whalebone covered with a thick layer of sod. Most houses consisted of a living area, an entrance tunnel, and one or more alcoves off the tunnel used for storage or other purposes. A ventilator shaft and a skylight (consisting of a framed rectangular hole covered with a translucent sheet made from seal intestines), both located in the roof above the living area, provided some temperature control and admitted some daylight. Only the living area had to be warm, and much of the required heat would be generated by the six to eight people who occupied it.

There were many variations in the basic sod-house model. In some regions houses were built with a single platform for sitting and sleeping purposes which would be located at the back of the house opposite the entrance. In other regions two or three separate sleeping/sitting platforms were built, sometimes in alcoves, at the sides and back of the open central area. Often two or three houses were connected to a single entrance tunnel. In the eastern Aleutians, in Labrador and in many parts of Greenland, the dwellings were long, rectangular structures which might house thirty or forty people, often an entire village.

The Polar Eskimos, who did not have access to wood or whalebone, made the framework of their sod- and snow-covered houses of stones piled up according

Within the Eskimo area, the largest ice fields and most numerous glaciers are in Greenland, although Baffin, Ellesmere and a few other islands in Arctic Canada also have significant ice cover. From there the land is essentially ice-free westward around the top of the continent to the Pacific Coast, where tall mountains and abundant precipitation create suitable conditions in some localities. This is the front of Childs Glacier, on Prince William Sound.

In the lush rain forests bordering Prince William Sound, in southcentral Alaska, the problem is not low temperatures but persistent wet weather and frequent storms. This is in sharp contrast to the desert conditions that prevail further north.

to the cantilever principle. The inhabitants of the islands in Bering Strait and of East Greenland also made extensive use of stone as a building material. In some parts of Alaska where timber was abundant, houses were built entirely of logs. Still another type of dwelling, sometimes built in parts of the Central Arctic, was the *qarmat*, which had a circular foundation of sod, stone or snow blocks, but a roof of skins. In northwestern Alaska many groups built a dome-shaped dwelling made of a frame of wooden poles covered by moss, skin or bark, or perhaps some combination of the three.

Substantial houses built of sod, wood, bone or stone justified the effort involved in their construction in regions where prolonged winter residence in one place was ordinarily possible, or where people returned to a particular location for a period each year. Elsewhere, a more easily constructed or else a portable dwelling was required. Tents could serve this purpose, and in some parts of Northwest Alaska where it was not too windy, they did. But in the Central Arctic, a region characterized by persistent strong winds as well as by low temperatures, tents provide poor shelter. The Eskimos' solution in this area was the famous dome-shaped snow house.

The material required to make a snow house is hard, wind-packed snow. Snow is comprised of tiny air pockets, which make it an excellent insulating material. If it has been packed into drifts under the proper wind conditions, it is also easy to extract and shape with the aid of a special knife. Suitable wind conditions were widespread only in the Central Arctic, which is the only part of the Eskimo world where snow houses were used as the ordinary winter dwelling.

The snow house dwellers – the Copper, Netsilik, Iglulik, Caribou and Quebec Eskimos – occupied an immense geographic area, but comprised less than eight per cent of the total Eskimo population.

A domed snow house was an architectural masterpiece, and it required considerable skill to construct. The builder had to know how to assess the properties of drifted snow, he had to be able to estimate the size of the ring for the foundation layer, he had to gauge the inward slope of the blocks so that they would converge at precisely the right place at the top without collapsing during the construction process, and he had to cut and shape each individual block without a template or other guide. Furthermore, he had to be able to do all of this in darkness, and in wind and bitter cold. Such skill took years of observation and practice to acquire.

Summer dwellings in most regions were skin-covered tents. These served as windbreaks, as shields from the usually light (though often persistent) northern rain, and as partial protection against the hordes of mosquitoes which infest much of the Eskimo world in summer. To keep the mosquitoes away, a smoky fire of scrub willows was built near the door. People often had to lie on the floor to keep from suffocating; but that was better than contending with mosquitoes. Northern summers seem unbelievably cold to people accustomed to warmer climates, but to Eskimos, temperature ranked a distant fourth to mosquitoes, rain and wind as an annoyance.

The third line of defence against the cold was artificially produced heat. In most parts of the Eskimo world this was provided by seal-oil lamps made from clay or soapstone. A properly trimmed lamp produced an odourless, bright yellow flame, and in most Eskimo dwellings one or two were sufficient to give off all the heat and light required.

But lamps were a hazard as well. Several recently discovered well-preserved bodies of pre-contact Eskimos in both Greenland and Alaska show evidence of a severe form of black lung disease, evidently acquired from inhaling too much sooty smoke from their lamps.

In many regions lamps were also used for cooking, which was done by suspending a pot containing water and chunks of meat or fish over the flame. In regions where oil was in short supply or where wood was abundant, cooking

The most common method of producing fire was a bow drill in which a 'bit' of hard wood was rotated very rapidly on a hearth of soft wood. The tinder used to catch the ember thus produced often consisted of the tassels of Arctic cotton, a plant common in tundra regions over much of the far north.

Facing page: Parkas had both utilitarian and symbolic features. This West Greenlandic woman's parka was made large enough for a mother to carry her baby on her back and swing it around to the front for nursing without ever exposing it to the elements. The front flap, reduced in size in this relatively recent model, symbolized the female reproductive system. Made of sealskin, this parka was decorated with strips of bleached skin embellished with pieces of dyed sealskin. In olden times the precise cut and trim would have indicated the wearer's nationality.

Below: Feet perspire more readily than most other parts of the body, and hence are particularly susceptible to frostbite. Caribou-skin insoles and dried grass or other good insulating material were used to keep out the cold. In Southwest Alaska grass was often braided into socks, such as these, to help deal with the problem.

was sometimes done over an open fire. Caribou Eskimos used to gather dwarf willows for the purpose, and cook their evening meals in alcoves located off the entrance tunnels of their snow houses. In much of Alaska they built a regular wood fire in a stone-rimmed hearth right in the middle of the living-room floor, opening the skylight to enable the smoke to escape.

The final line of defence against the cold, and ultimately the most powerful one from the Eskimo point of view, was magic. Faithful obedience to taboos by everyone in a settlement was the best way to increase the likelihood that frequent or prolonged storms would not strike during the winter months. Among the Western Eskimos, proper observance of the festival calendar also contributed toward that end. Certain charms, worn at appropriate places on the clothing, provided protection against cold for individual hunters and travellers. Shamans could assist by forecasting the weather, thus enabling people to anticipate a storm and postpone a hunt or a journey until it was over. Sometimes shamans attempted to control the weather by persuading their helping spirits to intercede on the people's behalf with the Spirit of the Air. Finally, shamans could ascertain the cause of a severe or prolonged period of stormy weather and prescribe measures to end it.

The various means the Eskimos employed to protect themselves against the cold were effective most of the time. But sometimes they were not, either through accident or because extreme cold or powerful winds simply overwhelmed them. Minor frostbite, especially of the face and wrists, was common. People were always looking for the telltale white patches on one another's cheeks which showed that freezing had taken place, and an individual travelling alone

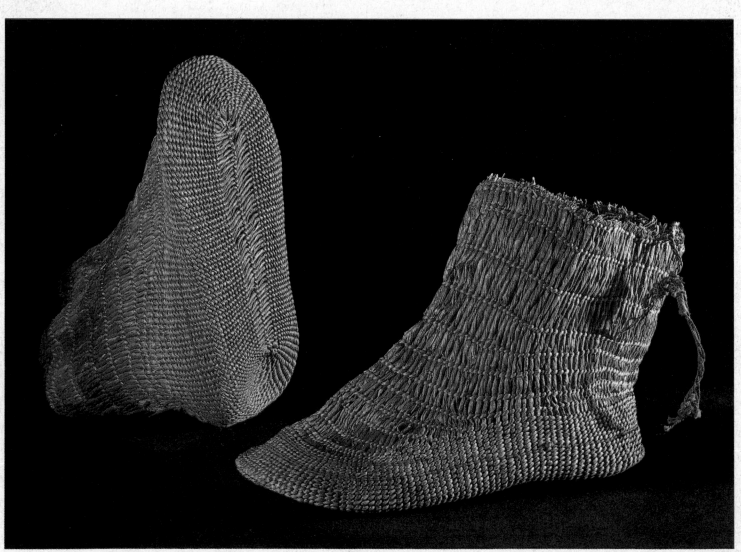

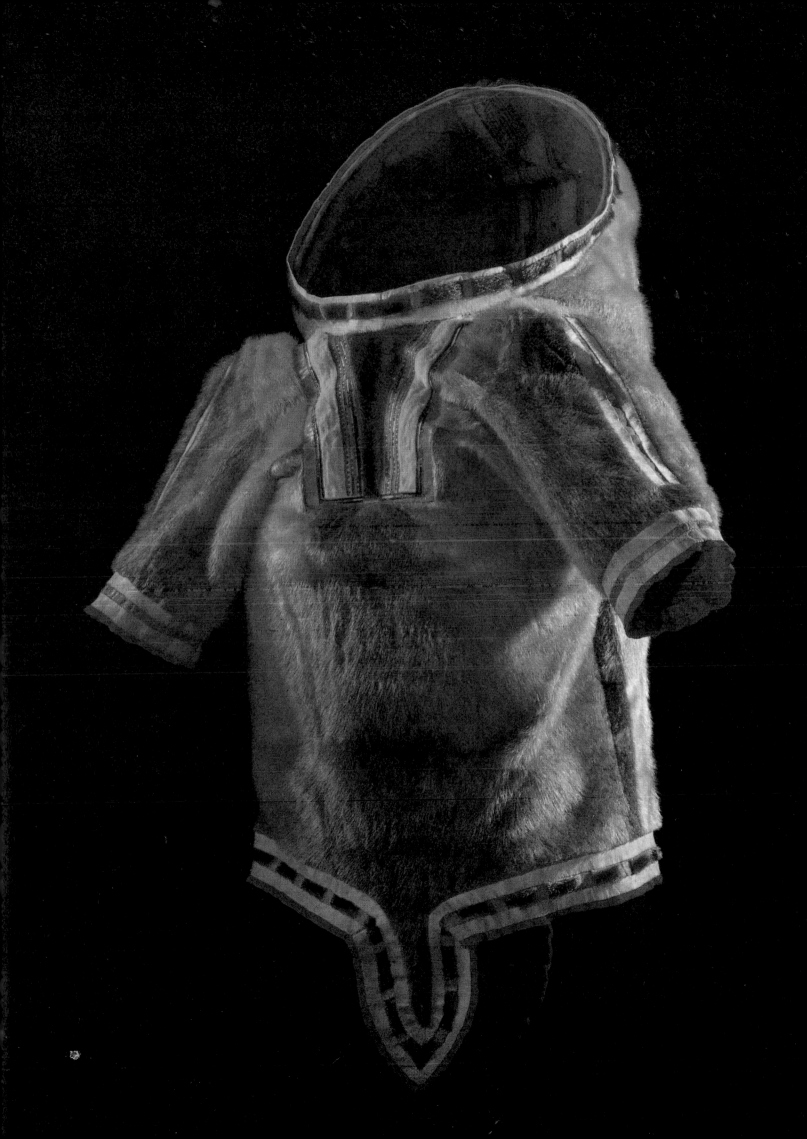

Kayak hunting on the open ocean is a dangerous enterprise. Hunters had to stay dry despite wind-blown spray or even capsizing, or run the risk of hypothermia. A waterproof sealskin parka, with tie cords around the wrists, face and waist, provided the necessary protection. Often the waist was fitted around the coaming that framed the hatch, thus fastening the hunter to his craft. An experienced boatman could capsize and right himself with a twist of the paddle without getting more than his face and hands wet.

wrinkled his face from time to time, any stiffness indicating the presence of frozen skin. All that was required to treat the problem was to remove a hand from a warm mitten and place it over the affected spot for a minute or two. If a foot froze, the common way of dealing with the problem was to remove one's boot and place the foot against a companion's stomach, which could be made accessible simply by pulling up the front of the parka, which would then be pulled down over the foot to keep it protected from the outside air.

Despite all their precautions, Eskimos occasionally experienced such severe frostbite that gangrene set in. Unless the affected part was removed, infection would spread throughout the body and result in death. The only recourse was to amputate. This usually involved removal of a finger or perhaps some toes, although occasionally an entire foot or hand had to be cut off. Fortunately,

Eskimos had expert knowledge of anatomy from their experience in butchering animals, and they knew how to sever a joint efficiently. The operation was agonizing, though, for they had no anaesthetic or other drug to alleviate the pain. Nevertheless, individuals are known to have amputated even their own frozen toes when survival depended on it.

The most dangerous condition of all was hypothermia, the reduction of overall body temperature. Unless quickly reversed, it leads to a person dying of shock, even if he does not actually freeze to death. Hypothermia was rarely a threat to Eskimos who had been eating well, whose clothes were in good condition, and who had access to shelter. If the clothing was in poor repair, if the people were caught outside in a severe storm, and particularly if they were starving, they were likely to die. Usually all three conditions occurred together. Starving people were too weak to mend their clothes properly, and, indeed, might even be eating pieces of it. They also would be more likely to risk setting forth in bad weather to try to reach another settlement or a cache of food.

The most common cause of hypothermia was falling into the water. In summer it could happen when a boat capsized, condemning its occupants to die in the frigid northern waters unless they could reach shore quickly. It is a tribute to Eskimo seamanship that this seldom happened. Falling through the ice in winter was a more common occurrence, especially with seal hunters. The hunter had to get out of the water quickly and roll in the softest snow he could find. The snow acted as a sponge, drawing the water out of the clothing. If this was done before the inner layer became soaked, and if the settlement was not too far away, the hunter would survive. Otherwise, he would die unless rescued by someone with clothing he could borrow. Nevertheless, the members of every coastal Eskimo group tell stories of incredible feats of survival by thoroughly soaked and chilled seal hunters.

Seal-oil lamps were used to produce heat in some parts of the Eskimo world and for light almost everywhere. Most lamps were made out of carved steatite (soapstone) or pottery, and lacked decoration. This unusual lamp of pecked stone features a seal apparently swimming in a pool of oil. The wick, of moss, was placed in the groove in the rim directly in front of the seal.

SUBSISTENCE

The greatest challenge to Eskimo survival was not the cold, but the difficulty of obtaining food, since the only food resources their country provides in any quantity are mammals and fish. These require considerable ingenuity and effort to obtain, not only because of the behaviour of the animals themselves, but because ice, wind and the barren landscape make it very difficult for hunters to approach their prey. However, once caught, northern animals and fish provided the raw material not only for food, but for clothing, shelter, fuel, utensils, tools and weapons as well.

The economy of most Eskimo groups was founded on sea mammals, of which quite a variety live in northern waters. At one extreme were several species of small hair seal, the largest of which weigh ninety kilograms (two hundred pounds). At the opposite extreme were several species of whale, the largest of which, the bowhead, can weigh more than sixty tonnes. Between them were large hair seals, fur seals, sea lions, walrus, belukha whales, narwhals, grey whales and humpback whales, the number and kinds varying from one region to another.

The same basic hunting technique was used for sea-mammal species in all parts of the Eskimo world. It relied on the use of the toggle harpoon, an ingenious device which resembled a lance, but which differed from it in important respects. Unlike a lance, the harpoon was used not for killing the prey but for attaching a line to it. This was crucial because even the smallest sea mammal is very difficult to kill with a single shot from a rifle, not to mention with a lance or a bow and arrow. A wounded sea mammal can easily escape beneath the water unless it is prevented from doing so by the very first object to strike it.

A hunter in his kayak had both a harpoon and a lance lying on the deck, held there by straps. A line about ten metres (thirty-three feet) long was attached to the harpoon head at one end, and to an air-filled sealskin float at the other. Most of the line was coiled on a small platform on the deck in front of the hatch; the float rested on the rear deck. The hunter propelled himself silently along with a (usually) double-bladed paddle, keeping a constant lookout for seals.

When he got within range of a seal he instantly picked up the harpoon with one hand and hurled it. The struck seal would dive, causing the harpoon head to separate from the foreshaft which, buoyed by the wood of the shaft proper, would float to the surface. Within seconds the diving seal would draw out the line on the stand and pull the float off the deck and under the water. From that point on, the seal was attached to the float, not to the hunter or to the kayak. This

Aleut hunters spent long hours in their kayaks on the turbulent waters of the north Pacific, often beyond the sight of land. Demonstrating exceptional navigational and boat-handling skills, they ventured forth to fish or hunt. This nineteenth-century model is made from baleen.

was a crucial safety feature because even a small seal can capsize a kayak if it pulls the boat in the wrong direction.

The hunter retrieved the shaft and foreshaft and waited. Initially, a seal could swim almost as fast pulling a float as it could without it. However, the expenditure of effort caused by the drag rapidly tired it, forcing it to return to the surface to breathe and rest. The float appeared first. As soon as it did, the hunter paddled rapidly towards the indicated spot, trying to arrive there just as the seal did. The frightened animal would dive again before recovering its breath. After a series of such manoeuvres it would become winded and exhausted, even though not necessarily badly wounded. Eventually, the hunter could paddle right up to the weakened animal and kill it with one thrust of his lance. He would then tie it to his kayak by a line, reorganize his equipment, and go looking for more seals.

The same basic principles used to hunt seals applied in most other sea-mammal hunting. The equipment used varied according to the size of the prey: the larger the animal, the heavier the harpoon and killing spear, the stronger the line, and the greater the number of floats.

Bowhead whales were too large for one hunter to take alone. In parts of the Eastern Arctic several men in kayaks hunted them in a group. Each would attempt to place a harpoon head into the whale so that the combined drag of several floats would exhaust it, forcing it to rest on the surface long enough for them to attempt a kill with their thrusting spears. This was not a particularly effective way to hunt whales because many were struck by just one or two small harpoons and managed to escape.

In Northwest Alaska, Asia and Greenland bowheads were hunted by crews of men using open boats, or umiaks. A standard crew consisted of eight men, including six paddlers, one harpooner and one helmsman. Each was able to concentrate on his specialized task, in contrast to the kayak hunter who had to propel and steer his craft, and handle the harpoon and lance all by himself. In a crew, the paddlers kept the craft moving at exactly the right speed, while the helmsman held it on course. The harpooner could make a precise and powerful downward thrust with a heavy harpoon, using both arms, from a standing position on the relatively firm base of the umiak. Instead of one or two floats,

Right: The mystical relationship between hunters and their prey is subtly expressed in this mask. What appears at first glance to be just a human face is both a man and a whale. A whale's tail and flipper serve as the man's nose and moustache; the top of a whale's head represents the chin, and its breathing hole replaces the mouth. Masks such as this were worn during ceremonies relating to the whale hunt. They served to increase both the chances of a successful hunt and the likelihood that the hunter would survive this dangerous activity.

which was all that could be carried conveniently on a kayak, three or four were employed from an umiak.

A third approach to whale hunting was used in the Pacific Eskimo area (and later by the Aleuts), where several different species of whales were to be found. A single kayak hunter attempted to place a light, poison-tipped lance into a whale. He immediately returned home and began a series of ritual procedures designed to kill the whale by magic, while other men in kayaks attempted to monitor the movements of the whale itself. As it swam about, the lance worked itself progressively farther into its body and the poison began to spread. If the lance had been properly placed, the whale eventually died. However, whales often expired far from where they had been struck, and those speared by hunters from one village were frequently recovered by those from another. But since the same hunting technique was employed everywhere, there was a supply of dead whales floating about over a very extensive area, ultimately yielding something for everyone.

In the Pacific Eskimo and Aleut sectors of Alaska, and in Southwest Greenland, the ocean never freezes; everywhere else the ocean is frozen for about half of each year. The presence of ice fundamentally altered sea-mammal hunting procedures, since it brought boat transportation to a halt. On the other hand, ice transforms the ocean surface into an extension of the land, so people can cross it on foot.

In general, sea ice did not severely hinder sea-mammal hunting. For groups who lacked boats, like the Polar Eskimos, ice actually enhanced it. Ice reduced the area in which a hunter had to strike his quarry. Sea mammals must breathe air directly, so the hunter had merely to wait beside a crack or breathing hole and try to harpoon a seal when it emerged to breathe. However, sea ice made it impossible to use a drag float, which meant that the hunter had to kill the seal with his initial thrust or he would be likely to lose it. The only reliable way to do this was to strike it squarely in the head, a very small and mobile target. The presence of ice also reduces the number of sea-mammal species available in most regions since the larger varieties migrate south of it for most of the freeze-up period. Except in a few areas where rip tides and currents keep the ice broken up, seals were the only sea mammals available to most Eskimos during the winter.

Breathing-hole hunting, which was the major winter seal hunting technique

Kayak decks were equipped with straps and racks to keep harpoons, spears, floats and lines in place, available for instant use. This float rack is adorned with four little seal figurines, which served both as decoration and as magical aids for hunting success.

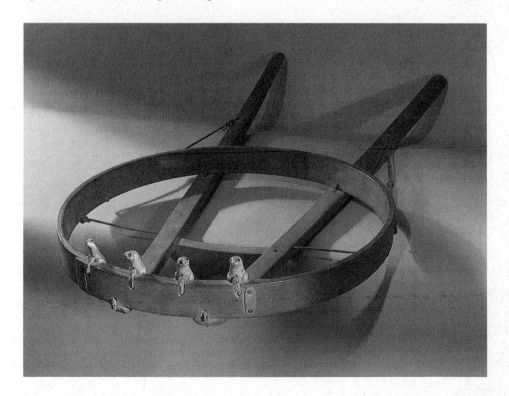

Left: When a harpoon-struck seal or whale became exhausted from pulling drag floats, it was dispatched with a lance. In contrast to a harpoon, the point was firmly attached to the shaft. Here we see the tip of a lance and the wooden sheath used to protect it when not in use.

Right: Seals are intelligent, curious creatures who investigate strange sounds. Hunters lured them to within striking distance of their harpoons by scratching on the ice with a device specially made for the purpose. This typical wooden scratcher (bottom) is divided into three 'fingers' to which bird claws are attached, and decorated with a blue bead. Just above it is a more elegant ivory model carved to represent a seal, with blue beads representing eyes and with seal claws attached to the base.

along the Arctic coast, was a much more demanding task than it might seem. First, the hunter had to locate a hole, which would be covered with snow and invisible at a short distance even to the highly practised eye. (Most Eskimo hunters took along a dog, whose nose provided a guide that no human faculty could duplicate.) Then the hunter waited, standing absolutely still in the bitter cold, for a seal to appear. This might not occur for hours or even days, since a seal normally has several breathing holes scattered over a wide area. When a seal does come up for air, it rises suddenly, without warning. The hunter, who might not have moved for hours, had to react instantly, thrusting his harpoon down through the snow at a target he could not see. And his aim had to be perfect, for seals do not offer a second chance. If the hunter moved prematurely, or if his aim was poor, the long wait in the cold would have been for nothing.

In the Central Arctic, where the sea ice is immobile for several consecutive months each winter, and where there are few alternative resources at that time of year, the Copper Eskimos raised breathing-hole hunting to a high art. First, they moved entire villages on to the ice, several kilometres from shore. When conditions were right, several hunters from each one went out together. The objective was to have one hunter at each of the holes existing in a particular locality. If a seal was frightened away from one hole before he took a breath, he would be forced to come up at another one nearby or suffocate. If every hole was guarded by a hunter, no matter where the seal emerged it was likely to be caught. One could never be sure that all the holes were guarded, of course, but the technique increased the chances of at least one or two hunters in a settlement getting a seal every day. Within a few weeks the local seal population would be depleted, and the village would have to be moved.

In the spring, when the sun starts to appear again in the north, seals crawl out on to the ice to warm themselves in its rays. They lie right beside the hole or crack

from which they emerged, raising their heads every minute or so to look around for danger. The only way a hunter can approach a sunning seal is to stalk it by crawling over the ice on his stomach, pretending to be another seal. When his intended quarry's head is down, the hunter inches forward, often through pools of frigid water if the spring thaw has commenced. When the seal raises its head, he either lies absolutely still, acting like a sleeping seal, or else he also raises his head and looks around, attempting to simulate the motions of a seal. Fortunately for Eskimo hunters, a seal's eyesight is not particularly good. A stalk might require several hours when carried out on flat ice, however, and there is never any guarantee that the quarry will wait that long. Eventually, if the hunter is lucky, he will approach within a few metres of his quarry and strike it with his harpoon.

A drag float cannot be used in ice hunting because the wounded seal will pull it under the ice, and both the float and the seal will be lost. The hunter therefore has to hold on to the harpoon line himself to keep his quarry from escaping. This is all right in the case of small seals, but one man cannot hold a large one for very long. So, in late spring when the larger varieties are present in some quantity in northern waters, a hunter usually took along an assistant. In the few regions where the much larger and more dangerous walrus was hunted by this technique, several people had to help.

Sea-mammal hunting, whether on water or on the ice, is an arduous enterprise, requiring patience, endurance and skill. It is also dangerous. The capricious northern weather is a constant threat to boat and ice hunters alike, threatening to capsize their frail craft or to break up the ice beneath their feet.

The larger sea mammals pose a direct physical threat to the hunter. Bowhead whales are relatively docile creatures compared to most species of whale, but they are so big that they can easily capsize a kayak or umiak with a mere flip of their tail. Humpback and grey whales, which are more common in the Pacific, in the Aleutians and off the Asiatic coast, are more likely to attack a small boat. Walrus can be quite dangerous. Although much smaller than a whale, a bull walrus can weigh more than an entire crew of eight men plus their boat and equipment. An annoyed walrus also does not shrink from attacking even a large boat, not to mention a man standing beside a crack in the ice. Since walrus frequently travel in pods of dozens or hundreds of animals, walrus hunting had to be conducted with considerable caution.

The most important land animal was the barren-ground caribou (or wild North American reindeer). Large populations of this species were found across the northern part of the mainland, while smaller herds existed in most of the ice-free parts of Greenland and on many of the Arctic islands of Canada. In some areas, such as the interior of Northwest Alaska, the barrens west of Hudson Bay and the inland portions of northern Quebec, caribou were the foundation of the entire economy.

Barren-ground caribou are always moving. There is broad regularity in their migrations, in that virtually all of them spend the summer on the tundra, and most of them pass the winter inside the tree line. Apart from that, their movements are very difficult to predict.

Over the millennia northern peoples learned how to turn the caribou propensity for movement to their own advantage. Instead of chasing after them, which is exhausting and usually unsuccessful, Eskimos simply ambushed the animals as they passed a particular point. The problem was to ascertain the route the caribou would take, so that the hunters could position themselves in time.

Hunters checked weather and game conditions continually to figure out where caribou might go. They also consulted their shamans, and they sometimes employed shamanistic intercession with the appropriate spirits to guide caribou movements in the most desirable direction.

They could never know for certain where the animals would go, but hunters could ensure that if caribou appeared in a given locality they would follow a very specific route. They did this by creating an avenue through which their prey would feel compelled to travel. When fording a river, when setting out to cross a lake, or when travelling through a range of hills or mountains, caribou have a natural preference for certain conditions, such as a shallow area in a river, the narrow part of a lake, or a wide valley through high hills or mountains. At such a place hunters constructed a sort of corral in the form of two converging rows of cairns (or piles of brush if rocks were not available) with the ground plan of a huge V. The narrow end of the V would be situated right at the shallows or other suitable place. The wide, or open, end of the V faced the direction from which the animals were most likely to approach at that time of year.

Once the cairns were in place, lookouts were posted. When caribou were seen approaching, people – often women and children – hid behind cairns near the outer end of the V, which could be a kilometre (over half a mile) or more wide at that point. After the animals entered it, the people stood up, shouted, and waved their arms. Sensing danger, the caribou would trot forward, moving farther into

Carvers rarely began work with a specific object in mind. Instead, they studied the blank, turning it over and over in their hands, until they discerned one or more images in the material itself. They then 'released' them by shaping the blank into those forms. Here we see a drag handle, which was attached to a loop of sealskin line and used to haul dead seals or other heavy objects across the ice or snow. These items were carved in a variety of forms out of wood, bone, ivory or antler, and considerable ingenuity was used in adapting their design to the shape of the raw material. This one has three heads; one is a seal and the other two are probably polar bears.

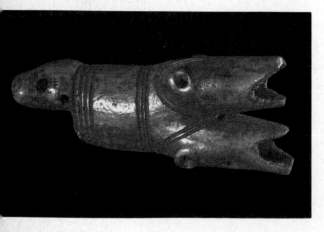

Right: This ingenious drag handle represents a seal rising to the surface to breathe. That figure is surmounted by a smaller seal that has just broken the water's surface and bent its head forward to look around.

Below: Predator-prey symbolism was well developed, the parallels between human hunters and non-human hunters being well understood and appreciated. These themes are captured in this West Alaskan charm, which symbolizes two species of hunter – human and polar bear – and their common prey, the seal.

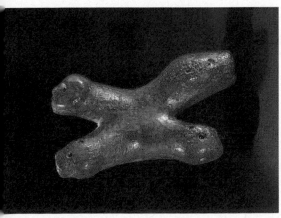

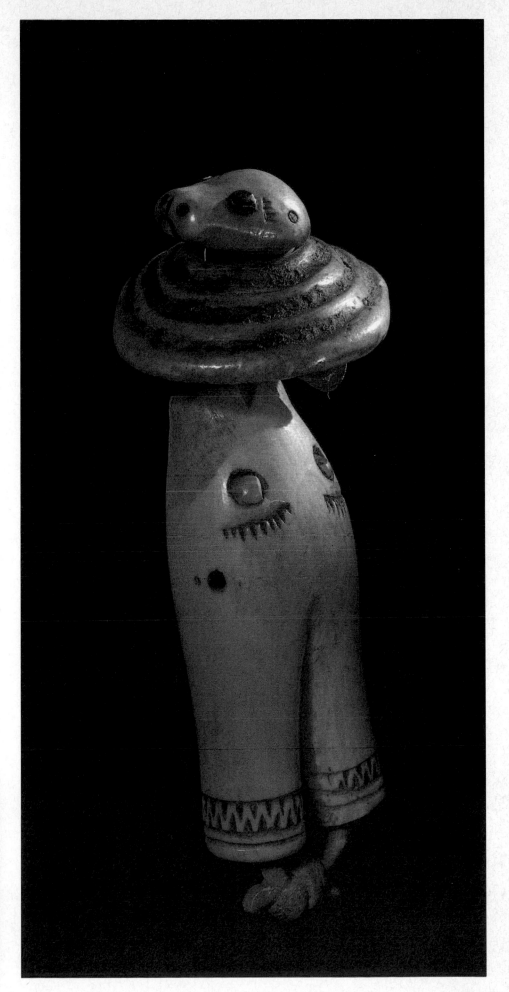

the V. They would mistake the cairns for human beings. This impression was reinforced from time to time by people hidden at different points along the way, who stood up and confronted any animals who hesitated or attempted to alter their course. As they approached the narrow end of the corral the by now thoroughly frightened animals were running right into a trap.

What awaited them depended on the circumstances. At a water-crossing they were met by lance-wielding hunters in kayaks. As the animals fled across the river or lake – and caribou are excellent swimmers – the hunters emerged from hiding places and speared them, usually killing them with one or two well-aimed thrusts to the kidneys. Since caribou are quite buoyant, dead animals would stay on the surface while the hunters pursued other prey. When they had all they needed, or when there were no more animals to hunt, the men would retrieve the floating carcasses.

When the corral did not terminate at a river or lake there were two alternatives. One was to attack the animals directly with lances or with bows and arrows. This was a poor method because it was frequently inconclusive. Wounded animals might escape, perhaps taking a valuable arrow or spear along with them.

A more definitive approach was to build a circular enclosure of stakes or cairns around the closed end of the V. As the caribou attempted to escape through the openings between the poles or rocks, they would be caught with snares made of heavy seal- or walrus-skin line.

Left: Stone cairns were used over much of the north as aids in driving caribou, who mistook them for hunters. In the level country west of Hudson Bay, from which this particularly realistic example came, cairns were also used as landmarks to aid winter travellers in finding their way across the nearly featureless frozen country.

Right: In northwestern Alaska crews of eight men hunted huge bowhead whales in small skin boats. Success in this dangerous enterprise depended upon a combination of superior equipment, technical skill and a variety of ritual observances designed to make the whales' spirits happy. All of these features are incorporated into this ivory bracket. It was lashed near the bow of the boat to hold the harpoon constantly at the ready. The whale effigy carved on the side was imbued with magical qualities that helped persuade the whale to yield itself to the hunters.

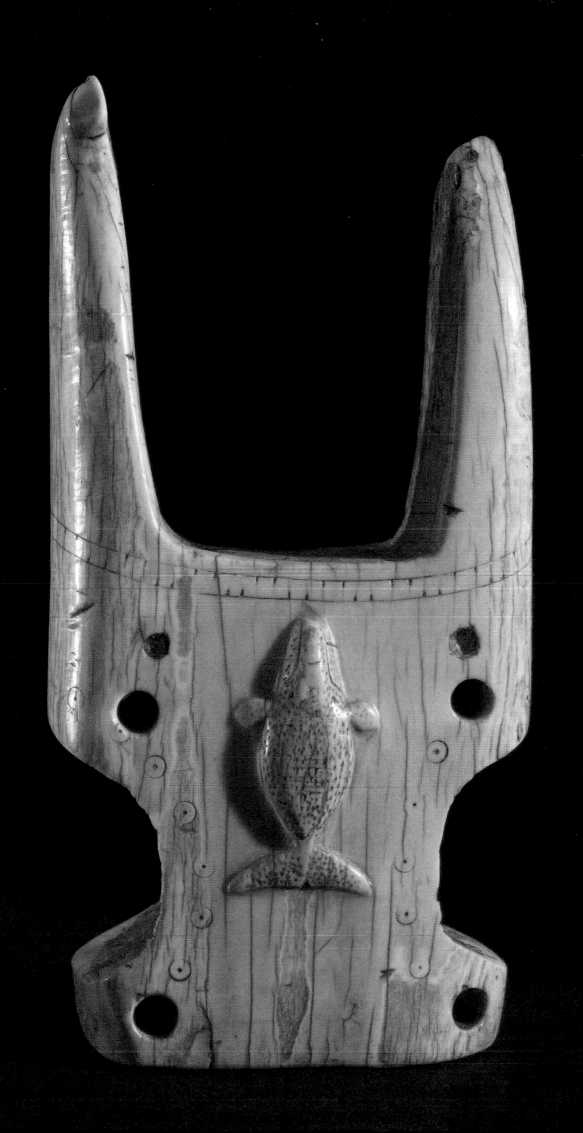

The corral technique was the most productive method for hunting caribou because it could yield dozens of animals at one time. Frequently caribou were too widely dispersed for it to work effectively, however, so other techniques had to be used. The most common alternative was to hunt them with bow and arrow. When they are travelling in large herds, caribou are remarkably easy to approach, and thus to shoot. When in small bands they are much more alert to danger, but even then they are not too difficult to get close to *if* there is no snow on the ground, *if* the wind is in the right direction, and *if* the animals are resting, chewing their cud or moving decisively in a certain direction. When any one of those conditions is not met, caribou are so difficult to approach that hunters usually did not waste their time trying.

In summer and early autumn caribou hunters spent a great deal of time just sitting. Usually they did so in small groups, on top of an eminence where they had a good view of the surrounding countryside. They talked quietly about the weather or their observations of animals, and worked on stone arrow points or spearheads. From time to time they set aside their work and gazed out over the landscape.

An Eskimo hunter peered fixedly in one direction for a prolonged period of time. He then turned his head slowly and slightly to one side, and repeated the process. He repeated it as often as necessary until the entire horizon had been scrutinized. The key to locating animals on the tundra is movement. Minor features in the distance appear as thousands of tiny dots arranged in a pattern that becomes progressively more obscure with distance; in summer, the pattern is often distorted by mirage effects. Animals, rocks and shrubs all appear as clusters of dots, but animals are dots that *move*! The best way for a hunter to discern this movement is to keep his own head absolutely still.

When the ground is covered with snow, caribou are visible at a considerable distance. Unfortunately, so are human beings. Furthermore, in very cold weather, snow becomes brittle and makes a loud crunching noise underfoot. When the temperature is very low the air is usually very calm; sounds carry over remarkable distances, so caribou often can hear a hunter even before they see him. They are thus particularly difficult to approach in mid-winter, the very season when they are most needed for food.

In winter most Eskimo caribou hunters had to rely on patience and warm clothing for success. Having observed at a considerable distance the direction of a caribou band's movement, the hunter stealthily proceeded to a hiding place some distance ahead of it. Then he sat and waited, perhaps for hours in the bitter cold, using a piece of skin to insulate him from the snow. He might build a screen of snow blocks to hide behind, and perhaps a windbreak as well. If the caribou continued on course, the hunter might get off two or three good shots from his bow before they escaped. If the animals changed course, then the hunter would have spent his time for nothing. If the animals were moving directly into the wind, as they often were, he might not bother trying to get them because they would get his scent as soon as he got in front of them.

When snow conditions permitted, caribou hunters dug pitfalls. They placed long, sharpened stakes at the bottom, then covered the hole with thin slabs of drifted snow. After urinating once or twice nearby, they left. Any caribou passing during the next several days would be attracted to the spot by the smell, fall through the cover, and be severely wounded or killed by the stakes at the bottom of the pit. The hunters could return at their convenience to retrieve the prey.

Still another approach was employed in Alaska, where there is an extensive growth of shrubs or trees along creek and river bottoms. Hunters cleared a trail through the brush and placed snares across it. Animals would be attracted to the trail because it offered easy passage, and be ensnared. This technique, like the pitfall, was an efficient way to hunt because men could be hunting caribou and doing something else at the same time.

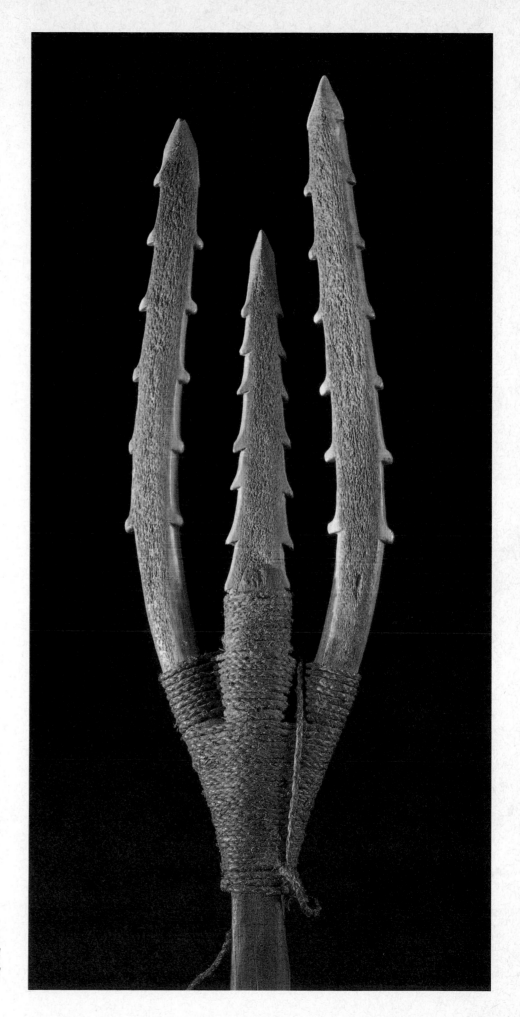

Left: In the central Canadian Arctic unusually pure and accessible deposits of copper enabled Eskimos to mine and use the mineral without subjecting it to a smelting process. This is a butcher knife with a blade of hand-beaten native copper and a handle made of two pieces of bone lashed together with sealskin.

Right: Most Central and Eastern Eskimos trapped migrating salmon or charr with stone weirs, then speared the fish with leisters. This Copper Eskimo leister has three points of antler lashed to a wooden shaft. The fish was skewered on the middle point, and prevented from slipping off by the side points and the barbs.

Fish were another important element in the Eskimo economy, particularly in Alaska, where they were the main source of food for many groups. Several varieties of fish live in northern waters, including lake trout, grayling, blackfish and pike in lakes and rivers; halibut, tomcod, capelin, herring and sharks in the ocean; and charr and several species of salmon and whitefish in both salt water and fresh. In Southwest Alaska eels are also common. The most important fish in most areas were salmon, charr and some kinds of whitefish, all of which make regular summer migrations from the sea into fresh water.

Eskimos employed the same general strategy against migrating fish that they used against caribou: they ambushed them. Fish are much more regular in their timing than caribou, however; and, in rivers at least, the location and direction of their movements are entirely predictable. The only variables fishermen had to worry about were rain, which raises the water level and makes fish inaccessible, and the size of the run, which in some regions can vary dramatically from one year to the next.

The weir and the leister were the main devices used to catch fish by the Eastern Eskimos. Fishermen built two rock dams across a shallow river or stream that salmon or charr were known to ascend during the course of their summer movement into fresh water. They left an opening in the downstream dam so fish could enter, but the upstream dam prevented them from going any further. When sufficient numbers were inside the weir, the opening was closed and people waded in and speared the fish with leisters.

In the Western Arctic, migratory fish were usually caught with nets, rather than with weirs, as they ascended the rivers. Nets were made from sealskin line in some areas, from shredded baleen in others, and from willow bark shredded and woven into line in still others. Making a net was a very laborious process, and sealskin and particularly bark nets were difficult to maintain, as they decay quickly if not properly cared for.

Net-making required the better part of a year. The raw materials were collected during the spring or summer. During the following winter, each woman made line of the appropriate calibre, then wove it into netting with the appropriate-sized mesh. The next summer, several women – fishing was women's work in most areas – attached their individual sections together to make a substantial net. In shallow rivers, nets were often used as seines to scoop up entire schools with a single sweep. In deep rivers they were usually employed as gill nets to trap individual fish as they moved up or down stream.

Pacific salmon die in the rivers after they spawn. Charr and Atlantic salmon spend the winter in the lakes and rivers, then descend to the sea again just after the

Left: These 1500-year-old ivory points were probably attached to the heads of bird spears. Three or four more points were usually attached to the shaft, just behind its midpoint. When hurled into a flock of birds from a range of up to 50 metres (over 150 feet), such spears sometimes impaled two or three birds at once.

Right: Winter fishing through holes chopped in the ice was often done by jigging. A bright lure – in this case a short string of beads – attached near the hook attracted the fish. It was moved up and down by jerking the short stick that served as a rod. A fish, attempting to bite the lure, was impaled in the mouth or lower jaw by the hook.

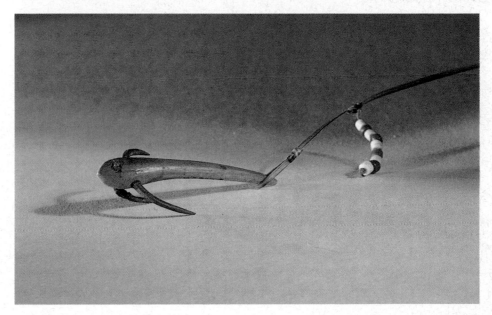

freshwater ice breaks up in early summer. The Eskimos did some fishing during this movement, but the combination of high water levels, floating ice and a seasonal preoccupation with sea-mammal hunting kept most Eskimo groups from conducting a major fishery during this period. In the Western Arctic, whitefish and also the strictly freshwater grayling make their down-river run in the autumn, beginning just about the time of the freshwater freeze-up. This run was aggressively harvested in many regions.

To harvest the autumn fish migration downstream, Alaskan Eskimos built fences across streams and small rivers. The work was facilitated by the fact that water levels drop significantly when rain is replaced by snow and when small tributary streams begin to freeze. A removable basket, or cage, with the opening facing upstream, was placed in a hole in the fence. A cone-shaped entrance was inserted into the opening, making it easy for fish to enter the basket but difficult or impossible for them to escape. After the initial labour involved in building the fence, the only work required of the fisherman was to empty the basket from time to time. The device could be used either until the fish stopped running, or until the ice got so thick that it became too difficult to operate efficiently. (In parts of Southwest Alaska this technique was also employed in reverse in summer, when the fish ascend the rivers.)

Many Alaskan Eskimos fished all winter long. The most productive technique was the gill net set under the ice. To set this net the fisherman chopped a series of holes, usually before the ice got very thick. He, or she, attached a long line to the end of a pole, thrust the pole down into the water, extended it beneath the ice to the next hole, and pulled it across. By repeating this process the fisherman could stretch the line any desired distance under the ice. He then attached the net to the line and pulled it under the ice as well.

Every day or two he would return, chop out the ice which had accumulated around the lines, pull the net out, and remove the fish and any debris. Sometimes little snow houses were built over the holes to insulate them from the cold winter air, thus reducing the buildup of ice. A wisely or fortunately placed gill net could produce a small but helpful supply of fresh fish all winter long while its owner spent most of his time on other matters.

Eskimos also fished with hook and line, and by dangling a lure in the water and spearing any fish which approached it. The simplest fishing technique of all was made possible by the fish themselves. Small Arctic cod, in parts of Alaska, and capelin, on the Atlantic coast, are periodically washed ashore by the tens of thousands. All the Eskimos had to do was scoop them up in baskets.

Eskimos hunted or gathered many other animals in as well as sea mammals, caribou and fish. Sea otters, musk-oxen, mountain sheep, grizzly bears, polar bears, foxes, wolves, lynx, marmots, wolverines, muskrats, ground-squirrels, beavers, river otters and hares were regionally or seasonally important resources, as were crabs, shellfish and sea urchins. In the spring and summer ducks, geese, gulls, cranes, swans and several species of sea-cliff nesting birds and their eggs were caught or gathered. In parts of Alaska, migratory waterfowl and their eggs were the only fresh food available for several weeks each spring, and snowy owls made a delicious addition to the soup menu each autumn, as they were caught during the southward migration. In many regions, the small, quail-like ptarmigan was a crucial source of fresh food in late winter.

Each species was pursued by means of specific techniques and weapons or other devices, such as snares or deadfalls, that centuries of trial and error had shown to be especially well suited to it. A hunter's kit contained not just one type of arrow but three or four, and not just one type of spear or harpoon, but as many as a dozen, each uniquely effective in capturing a particular type of mammal, fish or bird. Armed with superior equipment and a thorough knowledge of the habits of his prey, the Eskimo hunter harvested every animal and fish resource that his barren country had to offer.

Eskimos did not melt snow if they could avoid it. Snow consists mostly of air pockets, not water, and requires a tremendous amount of energy and time to melt properly. Ice, which contains much less air, was much preferred as a water source. Plain water was best of all, but it was often surprisingly difficult to get. Drinking tubes were used in winter as 'straws' when ice or debris in the water rendered other means of drinking unfeasible. In summer they were used during overland journeys to suck water from pools that were too shallow to get clear liquid from in any other way.

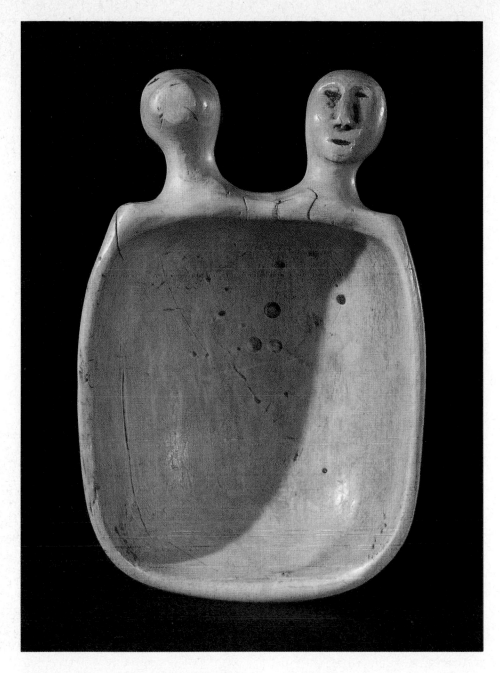

The migratory habits of their most important food resources meant that the
Eskimos had to accumulate large amounts of meat and fish during one or two
relatively brief periods each year, often during or just before the warmest season.
The greatest quantity of sea-mammal meat was obtained from May to July; in
many areas, most of the fish were caught from July to September, and the major
caribou kills occurred in August and September. But killing an animal was only
the first step. The Eskimos had to process, preserve and store all this meat for
consumption in leaner seasons. Fortunately, most of the work could be done at a
time when cold was not a problem and when it was light twenty-four hours a
day. When a bowhead whale was killed in May in a Northwest Alaskan village,
the entire population turned out to help butcher it, and haul the meat, blubber,
baleen and bone to the village. If they had to, the villagers worked continuously
for twenty-four, forty-eight, seventy-two hours or even more to complete the
job, sustained by frequent small meals of fresh meat and *muktuk* (whale skin with
attached blubber), and by the satisfaction of having their larder filled. They
would rest later, they said, during the long nights of the coming winter.

Most parts of the north are not cold enough to keep meat frozen all year
round, so preservation was a problem. Usually meat and fish were cut into strips

and dried in the sun or air for two or three days. The partially dried strips were placed in bags, or pokes, of seal blubber, which preserved them for at least a year if kept out of direct sunlight. The inhabitants of colder regions, such as the Polar Eskimos, who lived where the average temperature is above freezing for only a few weeks a year, simply eviscerated the game and stored the carcasses under rocks. The meat putrefied to some extent, but that only enhanced its taste as far as they were concerned. In Alaska they dug cellars into the permanently frozen ground. Meat placed inside quickly froze and was still suitable for human consumption two or three years later. Some meat was deliberately allowed to decay, however, for Eskimos regarded certain types of partially rotten meat as being very tasty; it was their counterpart of strong cheese. Rotten seal–flipper was considered a particular delicacy.

Blubber was an especially important commodity in most regions, and most groups who lived inland would trade for what they needed from people living on the coast. Blubber is a remarkable substance, one which fully justifies the paeans that most Eskimos offered in its praise. In texture it can be likened to beef fat which has somehow become fibrous and saturated with bacon grease. Unlike fat, it is self-rendering. Cubes of seal blubber put in a poke and kept out of direct sunlight for a month or two turn into a clear, nearly odourless liquid similar to vegetable oil, with a small, rubberlike residue at the bottom. Many Eskimos preferred oil with a slightly rancid taste, so they left some raw meat attached to the blubber, or placed the bag out in the sun for a few days.

Sea-mammal oil was a source of light, heat, medicine, food and food preservative. As fuel, it was placed in the bowl of a pottery or stone lamp. With a properly trimmed wick of moss or cotton-grass fibre it produced a surprising amount of heat and light. As medicine, consumed in excess amounts, it acted as a laxative. It was also rubbed on wounds or on irritated skin. As food, oil was either consumed directly as a beverage, mixed in soup, or taken as a sort of sauce with meat, fish, berries, or, in Alaska, with greens and roots. As a preservative, seal oil kept bacteria away from sun-dried meat and fish stored in it for a year or more. Oil was even used as insect repellent: rubbed on the face and hands of people and around the eyes of dogs, it helped keep the clouds of mosquitoes at bay during the warm summer months.

Every part of an animal was used, insofar as was possible. From sealskins Eskimos made clothes, boots, tent covers, boat covers, bags, pokes, floats, storage containers and rope. Caribou hides provided the material for lightweight but warm clothing, sleeping bags, and mattresses; they were made into tent covers and bags, and sometimes also boat covers and rope. Furs, bird skins, and even fish skins were made into clothing. Bones and antlers, and, of course, walrus ivory, were carved into the components of tools, weapons, implements, utensils, combs, needlecases, charms, ornaments and parts of masks.

Eskimos proved beyond any doubt that humans can be sustained by meat and fish alone. To do it, however, they had to consume not only the meat of each type of animal and fish that they killed, but also the blubber or fat, the eyes, the nutritious organ meats (especially the liver and kidneys) of the smaller sea mammals, fish livers, and the brain, tongue, heart, liver, kidneys, stomach, stomach contents, intestines and bone marrow of the caribou. They somehow managed to recover even the blood of most seals and caribou, consuming it either directly, as a beverage, or as an additive to soup. Finally, they drank copious amounts of water, a physiological necessity for people on such an extreme high-protein, low-carbohydrate diet.

The diet was often boring because it consisted of food that was available on a strictly seasonal basis. Fish (or seal or caribou meat) might comprise the entire menu for days. Eskimos thus looked forward to the berry season, which provided both welcome variety and valuable nutrition.

Eskimos did not dissipate the nutritional potential of their food by overcooking it. Great quantities of meat and fish were eaten raw, usually in either dried or frozen form. When they did cook their food they normally boiled it, usually lightly, and drank the broth. Eskimos occasionally died from starvation, but they never suffered from malnutrition.

Eskimos did not eat absolutely everything, for some northern foods are toxic. The accumulated experience of centuries told them what they should avoid as well as what they should seek. Experience did not protect them completely, of course. They did acquire diseases, and especially parasites, from animals. Although only a few were fatal, several were debilitating.

Vegetable products entered the economy in various ways. Berries, leaves, roots, seaweed and greens were valuable additions to the diet in many areas, especially in Southwest Alaska. In the Western Arctic generally, certain types of root, leaves and bark were used for medicinal purposes and as colouring agents, and bark was used to make line for nets. Most groups in southwestern Alaska also used grass to make several different kinds of mat and basket, the Aleuts carrying work in grass to a particularly high level of craftsmanship. Processing (cleaning and drying or cooking) and storing vegetable products often took as much time and effort as that required for fish and game. In most areas, both the collection and processing of vegetable products other than wood was done exclusively by women.

Wood was the most important vegetable resource in the north. In the Aleutians, and in most coastal areas everywhere else, it was available only in the form of driftwood. On the barren shores of Alaska and Asia driftwood was available in abundance, having been brought to the sea by several great rivers and carried northward by ocean currents. In the Central Arctic and in Greenland, even driftwood was rare. Some groups in the Central Arctic periodically made long journeys south for wood, while others obtained wood by trading for it with

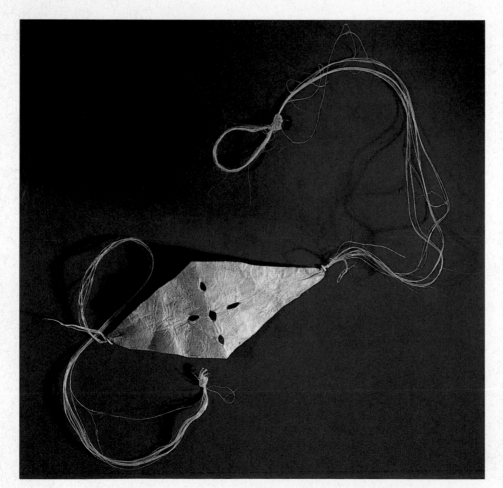

Left: Countless generations of Eskimo boys learned the rudiments of hunting by stalking and attempting to kill shore birds with slingshots. These alert creatures are not easily approached, however, and aspiring young hunters often spent hours crawling on their stomachs through mud and grass only to have their quarry fly away before they could take a shot.

Right: Wind-packed snow is difficult to shovel, but easily cut and shaped with a knife. Snow blocks were probably used to make windbreaks and storage platforms long before the snow house was invented. This snow knife is made from three pieces of ivory lashed with sinew.

people who were better situated. The Polar Eskimos of northwestern Greenland had to do without wood of any kind.

Wood was used in constructing house frames, tent poles, boat frames, paddles, oars, sleds, bows and arrows, spear-throwers, sun-goggles, masks, spoons, and harpoon and spear shafts. In some regions it was used to build grave scaffolds, and to make hats, sunshades, buckets, dishes, trays and boxes. The most extensive and skilled work in wood was in southwestern Alaska where, in addition to its other uses, it was employed in elaborate mortuary art which included coffins and several types of monument and effigy.

Few Eskimo groups used wood as fuel. It was too valuable, and they had an excellent alternative in sea-mammal oil. Groups who had no wood of their own, and who could not acquire it through trade, had no boats, tents, or bows and arrows. Their houses were constructed of rock, whalebone or snow, and their sleds and harpoon shafts were made from many pieces of bone and ivory, painstakingly shaped and pinned or lashed together.

Eskimos had few but important requirements for mineral products. Flint, slate and other appropriate rocks were flaked, chipped or ground into harpoon and spear heads, arrow points, knives and adzes. Most of the raw material was either simply picked up from the ground surface, or acquired through trade. Western Eskimos made their lamps and pots out of clay. Eastern Eskimos, lacking clay, constructed lamps and pots out of steatite (soapstone), a heavy rock which had to be quarried, but a relatively soft substance that is easily extracted and shaped.

Through hard work and the expert knowledge acquired over several thousands of years of trial and error, Eskimos made their barren land provide. The Eastern Aleuts, along with some of the other Western Eskimo groups, may even be said to have lived fairly comfortably. But in other regions, such as the Central Arctic and the northern and eastern parts of Greenland, Eskimos had a difficult life indeed.

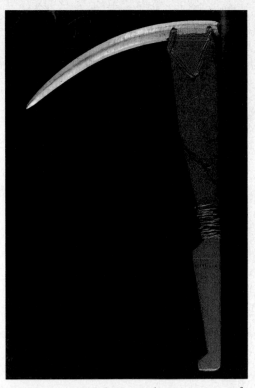

Above: Western Eskimos made extensive use of the roots of different plants for food, medicine, dye and paint. They were dug up with picks such as this one from northwestern Alaska. It was made of a walrus tusk point lashed to a wooden handle. The butt end of the handle is carved in the shape of an animal head.

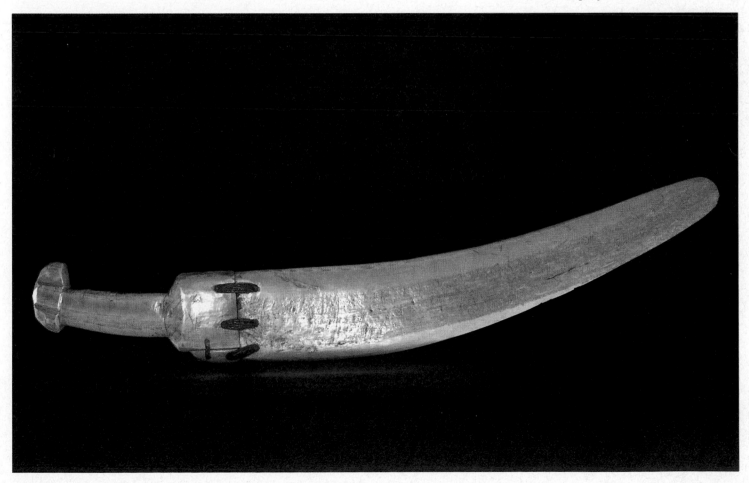

MOVEMENT

Most Eskimos, being dependent on migratory animals and fish, had to move themselves at least twice a year; they had to move to where the animals were or do without. In some regions, they had to go only a kilometre or two between summer and winter settlements; in others, they had to make several dozen moves and traverse hundreds of kilometres of countryside each year. Only the Asiatic and a few Southwest Alaskan and Pacific Eskimo groups seem to have been able to stay in one place all year round.

Some of the many considerations involved in Eskimo movement can be illustrated by a description of a specific case. The *Napaaqturmiut*, or Lower Noatak River people, were a small Northwest Alaskan group of about 250 whose territory consisted of a large flat area along the lower Noatak River (which flows into the Chukchi Sea just north of the modern town of Kotzebue), the edge of some high mountains bordering the flat to the east, a range of hills west of the river, and a portion of the sea coast just beyond that. The society derived its Eskimo name, which means 'people of the spruce', from stands of trees growing along the river and the lower slopes of the nearby hills. Away from the river most of the country is covered by tundra vegetation, although the creek bottoms have substantial thickets of willows and alders as well.

In late December the Lower Noatak people ordinarily were distributed in a number of small settlements of sod and log houses in the forested area adjacent to the river. They lived on fish and sea-mammal supplies obtained the previous summer, on caribou meat acquired the previous autumn, and on such fish and game as they had recently acquired near the river itself. The latter consisted primarily of caribou; charr, grayling and ling cod caught through holes chopped in the river ice; and ptarmigan and hares snared, netted or shot in the willows.

The people remained in these settlements all winter long if the game supply in their vicinity was sufficient. If the supply of food became inadequate, as it usually did in January, the people had to seek better hunting grounds. Just where they went depended on the judgements of the various family heads about where game would be found. The decision varied from year to year, and from family to family. In any case, as food supplies ran out, families began to leave the few, relatively large settlements of autumn, and establish a larger number of smaller settlements scattered over a much wider area.

The family head was the one to make the decision to move, but he normally did so after discussion with the other adult members of the family, and often after

In northern latitudes long periods of twilight characterize the short days of early and late winter. Sunrise merges into sunset, and the gorgeous panoply of colours is reflected off the snow-covered landscape for several hours at a time.

consulting a shaman. The large extended families of autumn had to divide into smaller units at this time. The members of each sub-family loaded their sleeping bags, extra clothing, utensils and food on to two or three sleds and set out in a direction its leader judged most promising. Any possessions not needed in winter were left behind. This was not a time of joy, for scarcity had forced them to move, and a period of even greater hardship probably lay ahead.

A typical party consisted of an old woman, her two grown sons and a daughter, and their respective spouses and children – perhaps twelve or thirteen people. One man, wearing snowshoes, walked ahead, breaking a trail through the deep, soft snow. The three sleds, arranged single file behind him, each bore a load weighing some 225 kilograms (496 pounds). The harnesses of the two or three dogs pulling a sled were attached directly to it by a line one to three metres (three to ten feet) long. The women and any teenage children helped pull the sleds, drawing somewhat longer lines that ended in chest straps. Infants travelled in the backs of their mothers' or older sisters' parkas. Toddlers rode on top of the loads, and youngsters walked behind. The grandmother rode or walked, depending on her strength and on travelling conditions. The other two men and one of the women or older boys pushed and guided the sleds from behind. Progress was slow, maybe a kilometre or two (about one mile) per hour, if the trail was not previously broken. Once or twice they paused to rest or have a snack of sun-dried or frozen raw fish and seal oil.

In the afternoon the party stopped and created a brand-new settlement, erecting two or three round, dome-shaped houses by stretching caribou-skin covers over willow-pole frames. While the men and older boys walked to the nearest hill to look for signs of caribou in the waning daylight, the women and older girls arranged the houses. They spread willow branches on the floor around a central hearth as insulation from the snow, covered the mats with a layer of caribou hides, moved all the sleeping bags and other gear inside, and lit the lamps. They were now prepared to stay there for one night, or for three months, as circumstances might dictate.

If signs of ptarmigan or hare had been observed, the women and older children set snares in the nearby willow thickets before it got too dark to see what they were doing. The dogs were then unhitched. Each was fastened to a willow bush or spruce tree by means of a collar attached to a length of wood, which was connected at the other end to a short line tied to the bush or tree; with such an arrangement a dog could not chew its way free. If possible, the seven or eight dogs were arranged around the houses to serve as sentinels. They were then fed their daily meal of frozen or dried fish, caribou or seal meat, and oil or blubber.

The people's evening meal was the same as the dogs', except that it was ordinarily lightly cooked. If they had been lucky that day and someone had killed a hare or some ptarmigan they ate the fresh meat instead. A fire of dried willows or spruce branches was made in the central hearth, and three or four rocks were placed in it. By the time the men returned from their survey, the rocks were extremely hot. One by one, they were placed in a large wooden bowl containing pieces of meat or fish, and water, which had been obtained from the river through a hole chopped in the ice. By the time the fourth hot rock was in the pot, the water was boiling, and by the time the broth was cool enough to drink, the meat was considered cooked. In one of the houses, the men and older boys were served the meat or fish on a wooden tray and the broth in wooden bowls. The women and children ate separately, in the house where the food had been cooked.

After dinner, the men might spend an hour or so making or repairing tools or weapons, and discussing what they had seen that day and their plans for the next, while the women mended and dried clothes and chatted in the other house. Or the entire group might gather together in one of the huts to sing, to hear the grandmother tell stories, or to play games. (If they expected to stay in one place for any length of time, they built a 'kashim' in which such community activities were held.) Periodically, someone would step outside to look around.

Whenever it became uncomfortably cool, the skylight was opened, a fire lit beneath it, and rocks placed inside. When the rocks were hot enough and the fire died down, the remaining embers were tossed out the door, and the skylight was closed. The rocks continued to provide radiant heat for quite some time afterwards.

Eventually, after the men made a final check of the weather and people had attended to their toilet needs, they crawled into their sleeping bags. The lamps were put out or trimmed, the members of the settlement dropped off to sleep, and the monumental quiet of the arctic night descended on them.

The adults began to stir about six o'clock the following morning, well before dawn. The men went outside to check the weather and generally look around,

Frequent moves required portable containers, and the paraphernalia of every household included storage bags of diverse sizes and shapes. This nineteenth-century Aleut bag is made of strips of walrus intestine decorated with coloured pieces of cloth obtained from Russian traders.

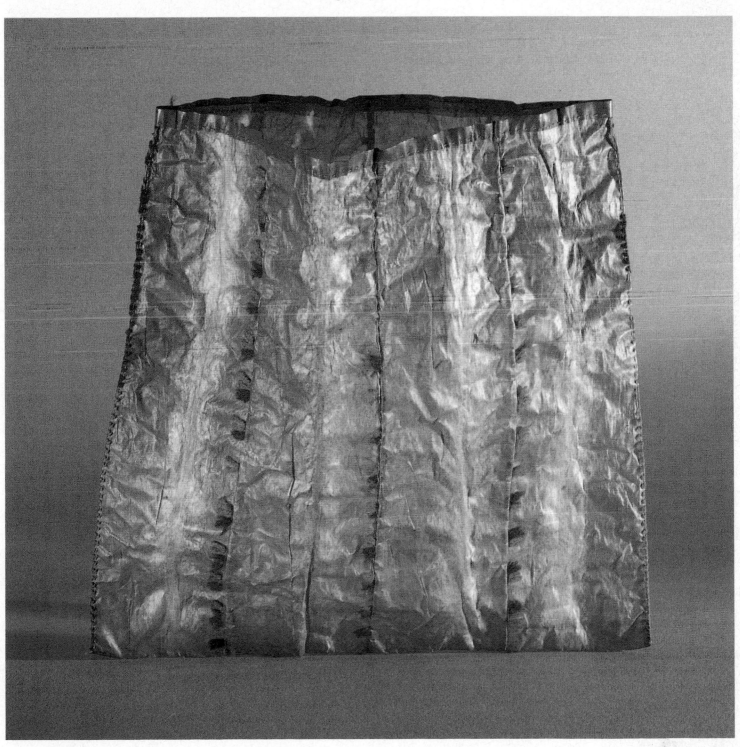

while the women cut up some frozen fish for the morning meal. The children were then aroused to join the others for a breakfast of frozen raw fish and seal oil. The dogs were not fed unless it was bitterly cold, in which case they received some blubber and possibly a piece of meat or fish. After breakfast, the children checked the snares, and everyone helped pack for the coming day's journey. By the cold light of the young day, about 8.30 or so, they were on the trail, pushing onward in their search for food.

This process was repeated as often as necessary until the family arrived at a productive hunting ground. Usually they stayed near the river because small game and ptarmigan were more likely to be found there in the heavy willow growth, and because fish might be caught through holes chopped in the ice, which was by now a metre (over three feet) or more thick. If they succeeded in killing some caribou, or in making an especially good catch of fish, they stayed in one place and lived relatively comfortably for a few days. Often, however, all they had to sustain them during February and early March were a few scattered ptarmigan and hares.

If there was a death along the way, the deceased would be left in the snow, or placed on a hastily erected scaffold. If someone fell ill or was injured, that person would have to be carried on the sled, hindering the party's progress. If a pregnant woman felt birth pains coming on, a small parturition hut would be built for her, and she would be placed in it, along with a small supply of food. If there was a good camping place nearby, the rest of the party would halt there. Otherwise, they would continue on until they found one. The mother would bring her baby into the world alone – as she would have done anyway in accordance with local custom – and catch up with the rest of the party later, on foot, carrying the newborn infant inside her parka.

Moving required a tremendous amount of work and involved a certain

Winter travel was facilitated by the use of sleds, the size and shape of which varied according to local custom and the available wood supply. Polar Eskimos had very little wood, so to make this late nineteenth-century sled they had to combine several small pieces of wood and ivory, and carefully shape and lash them together with sealskin rope. The runners are shod with strips of ivory. It is shown equipped for a hunting expedition with two harpoons, a coil of line and other equipment tied on it. Prior to the arrival of Europeans in the region, the Polar Eskimos had to make their sleds and their weapons entirely of bone and ivory.

Right: Wicks for seal-oil lamps were made of moss, a supply of which had to be kept clean, dry and available for use when needed. In many regions it had to be collected in summer or autumn and stored for the winter. Here we see an unusual moss storage bag from East Greenland that was made from seagulls' feet and bleached sealskin, decorated with an appliqué design made from strips of unbleached sealskin. Appropriately enough, the design symbolizes the sun or, more generally, light.

amount of risk. But when food supplies were low, it was even more dangerous *not* to move. The only thing that could prevent movement was inclement weather, which meant strong winds and blowing snow, not cold as such. When a severe storm struck, there was nothing the people could do but stay in their houses and wait until it was over. Sometimes the men could not hunt for a week or more. If food supplies were low to begin with, such a delay could be disastrous. Even if the people survived the storm itself, they might be too weak afterwards to travel. It was then that the bones saved from animals consumed during the previous months were boiled to yield any residual fat they might contain, and even some of the skin clothing might have to be boiled and eaten. In the Lower Noatak region, however, although late winter was often a lean time, it was rarely severe enough for people to die.

The middle of March signalled the approach of a new season. It is still cold on the lower Noatak at that time of year – sometimes as low as -40° centigrade (-40° Fahrenheit), or even colder – but the days are getting longer. The people knew that seals were beginning to crawl out on the ice of the Chukchi Sea to sun themselves, and that they would be spending progressively more time doing so with each passing day. They also knew from long experience that any caribou in the region would soon begin to move north to the far side of the mountains, and that in May and June most of the fish would leave the river. Even if there were enough ptarmigan and hares along the river to keep their stomachs full during the early spring, the people realized that they would not yield a supply of meat and fat sufficient for the following autumn and winter. Finally, they understood that they could not afford to wait for these developments to occur before they made their next move. Once all the fish and game had gone, it was too late.

Anticipating developments they knew were inevitable, the *Napaaqturmiut* returned to their autumn settlements to retrieve the rest of their gear. They loaded

This West Greenlandic storage bag was made from pieces of bleached, dyed and untreated sealskin sewn together with overlapping (double) seams to make it waterproof for boat travel. It is decorated with an appliqué design of pieces of sealskin.

their large travelling boats, or umiaks, on to flat sleds, and loaded them with all the other paraphernalia they would need over the next several months, which meant practically everything they owned. Then they headed west, over the hills, towards the Chukchi Sea coast.

If the winter had been good, so that people and dogs were well fed, and if the trail was fast, this move would be accomplished in just a day or two in an atmosphere of great anticipation. If, on the other hand, people and dogs were starving, or if the snow was very deep, the move would be an increasingly grim effort that might require as much as two weeks to complete. In either case, it had to be undertaken if life was to go on.

When the *Napaaqturmiut* arrived at the coast in late March or early April, they found the Chukchi Sea covered with an ice pack extending the whole way to Asia. Since the water near the Alaskan shore is shallow, and since the current is

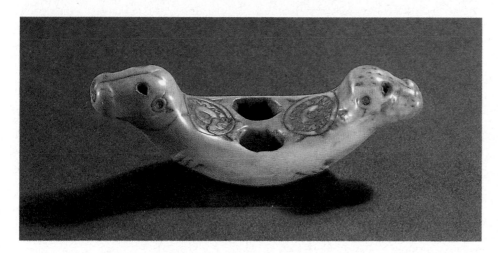

Left: Seals, so crucial in the economy of many Eskimo societies, are neatly represented in this ivory belt fastener from western Alaska.

Below: One reason that traditional Eskimo carvings were small is because large ones would have been too burdensome to carry as people moved around during the course of their annual cycle. This small ivory image of an East Greenland man is a good example. The large soapstone sculptures familiar to Westerners as 'Eskimo art' were not produced at all until after European contact, and not in any volume until the mid-twentieth century.

weak along Lower Noatak territory, the ice there is normally stable in early spring. The people left their boats, tents and other equipment on the shore, and moved right out on to the frozen ocean. They remained there for several weeks, living in small, rectangular snow houses, until the ice began to melt and break up with the advancing season. The men hunted seals – especially the large bearded seals – and the women processed the meat, and hauled it, with the aid of dogs and sleds, to the place where their equipment was stored on shore. By late April there is at least some light all night long at this latitude, and the spring seal-hunting period was a time of intense activity.

When the ice began to break up, the *Napaaqturmiut* moved ashore. There they lived in dome-shaped tents in small camps situated at the mouths of streams scattered along about fifty kilometres (thirty miles) of coast. As the break-up process proceeded, the men continued to hunt seals, first on the ice, later by kayak, and ultimately, for a brief period, by umiak.

Eventually the break-up process reaches a point at which boat travel is possible. The people in the northernmost Lower Noatak camp then packed all of their belongings into the umiaks, including sleds, kayaks, and their newly acquired stores of seal meat and blubber, and headed south along the beach. When they reached the next camp, they were joined by its inhabitants. The combined party continued down the coast, growing every time it came to a new camp. By the time it reached the last one, the entire membership of Lower Noatak society was travelling together in a flotilla of fifteen to twenty umiaks. After a winter and spring of isolation and at least some hardship, this particular move proceeded in an atmosphere of great festivity and a general sense of well-being, with people laughing, talking and singing as the dogs towed their boats along the beach.

The *Napaaqturmiut* halted and erected a new village on a stretch of beach on the north shore of Kotzebue Sound known as Sisualik, 'the belukha (white whale) place'. Already established a bit farther on was a similar but somewhat

larger settlement of Kotzebue *(Qikiqtarzungmiut)* people, and a bit beyond that, on the point, was the Upper Noatak *(Nuataarmiut)* camp. A few families of Kobuk Delta *(Kuungmiut)* people might be encamped there as well. Altogether, there were more than a thousand people living along this one stretch of beach. In kayaks, the men from these societies hunted belukha, which congregated here in large numbers early every summer.

The number of people at Sisualik was swelled further after the sea ice left the coast in July, as boatloads of people from several other societies – some from as far away as Asia – converged on the spot for the great summer fair. The Sisualik fair was the largest regular gathering of Eskimos in the world. It consisted of two thousand or more people who came together every summer for feasting, trading, dancing and athletic competition, as well as for the Eskimo equivalents of diplomacy, espionage and foreign intrigue. It was an extraordinarily exciting time for the people involved – joyful, for the relatives and partners they would meet, tense for the enemies who were there.

The fair began to break up after about two weeks, since such a large number of people and dogs could not be sustained for long even at Sisualik without depleting the supplies accumulated for the following winter. Besides, people wanted to return to their respective countries for the late-summer fishing and hunting seasons. The *Napaaqturmiut* loaded their by now substantial stores of seal and belukha meat and blubber into their umiaks and proceeded up the Noatak River, which enters Kotzebue Sound just east of Sisualik. They ascended it to their own country, immediately to the north of Kotzebue society territory.

August and September were spent in fish camps, where teams of women seined for salmon, charr and whitefish. Parties of men travelled farther upstream by umiak to where the mountains converge on the river. They hid their boats and walked north or east into the mountains looking for caribou, whose hides are in prime condition for clothing at that season. The hunters cached the meat under rocks, and packed the hides of any animals they killed down to the boats, usually with the aid of dogs. When enough had been obtained, or if freeze-up appeared to be imminent, they headed back downstream to rejoin their families.

While the freezing process was in progress and movement of any kind was dangerous, sometime between mid-September and mid-October, the Lower Noatak people built new sod or log houses, or cleaned up their old ones. Usually

Less obliged than their northern and eastern cousins to make protracted and frequent journeys, the people of Southwest Alaska were able to accumulate goods in greater quantity and variety. This, in turn, required more storage facilities. This wooden trinket box shows, carved in relief, a salmon, the primary resource that made this more sedentary life possible.

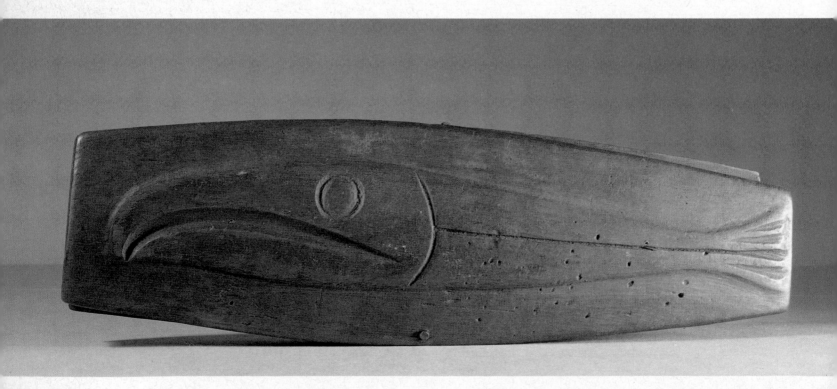

they were located close to the fish camps. The comparatively large settlements in which these houses were located served as their homes for the autumn, and often for part of the winter as well.

During the autumn months the *Napaaqturmiut* were usually sedentary. Food supplies were at their peak, and such large stores could not be moved easily once the ice prevented boat travel. Using sleds and dogs, the men retrieved any meat they had cached earlier in the mountains, and hunted caribou closer to home as opportunity presented. The women and children, meanwhile, set snares for ptarmigan and rabbits. As soon as the rivers froze, they set weirs and fish traps under the ice, and also hooked for fish through holes chopped in the ice.

Autumn was the main time for warfare in Northwest Alaska. It was the season when new or old grudges against nearby peoples were remembered and, from time to time, settled. Since food supplies were good, the men could afford to stop hunting for a while without fear that their families would starve. The rivers, lakes and marshy ground are sufficiently frozen to permit overland travel, yet the snow is not yet deep enough to hinder movement. There is still enough light to permit comfortable daytime walking, but also enough darkness to conceal a night-time raid. Any major moves at this time of year were ordinarily made only by parties of armed men, travelling light and moving on foot. Sometimes they travelled remarkable distances, too; even a distance of, say, 500 kilometres (300 miles) one way was not a deterrent to an aroused group of warriors.

Autumn was also a time for defence. This was one of the reasons that autumn villages tended to be relatively large. Any attacking force would have to penetrate a sentinel screen of several dozen dogs, then run the risk of being met by an equal number of forewarned, armed defenders.

During the short days of December and early January, extensive movement by Lower Noatak people, including raiding-parties, ceased. Food supplies were

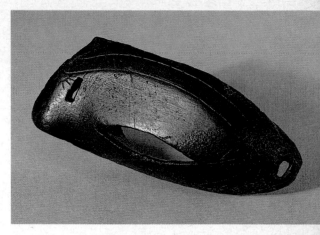

Above: Around the middle of March the returning sun begins to produce a glare on the snow-covered landscape, especially north of the tree line. By late April the country is like a giant mirror, reflecting the ever more direct light. People out in this environment suffer severe pain and even blindness if their eyes are not very well protected. These broken 1800-year-old goggles represent an early attempt to deal with the problem.

Left: This remarkable ivory drag handle represents two belukhas (white whales) tied together on their stomachs and pierced through the middle for receiving the ends of the cords. The latter project from their mouths, and originally formed a loop. Both figures are lashed to ivory chains, one of which is attached to a small carving in the shape of a belukha's tail.

still good, but travel was more difficult, and daylight was too brief for hunting to be very productive. This was their holiday season, a time when families in neighbouring villages got together for several weeks of visiting, dancing, feasting, games and other communal activities.

Sometimes the holiday period saw a great deal of movement, however. This occurred when allied families in different societies invited one another, by messenger, to visit them for a general celebration. Although typically referred to in English as a single event, 'the messenger feast', it actually consisted of a whole series of feasts, dances, rituals, games and other activities spread over a period of a week or more. The journeys involved might be just as extensive as those associated with warfare, but they were undertaken by extended families, not by small groups of men. Instead of travelling with a minimum of supplies, they ventured forth laden with food and other gifts for their hosts. Depending on

how far apart the hosts and their guests lived, the combined round trip and festivities could take as much as six weeks to complete.

When the holiday season ended, usually in early to mid-January, the surplus of early autumn was exhausted. Once again, it was time for the winter dispersal.

The movements of the Lower Noatak people were representative of Eskimos generally in that several had to be undertaken each year in order to ensure survival, and in that they followed a regular pattern from one year to the next. This pattern included some periods inland and others on the sea coast, giving them direct access to both terrestrial and marine resources. Most characteristic of all is the fact that most of the moves were made by family groups travelling with full equipment. Every time they stopped, even for one night, they established a new settlement. When Eskimos travelled they tried to be prepared for any eventuality, for they knew from painful experience that trips intended to last for only a week or two could turn out to last for months or even years.

The movements of the Lower Noatak people were unusual in being more regular than most. They did not spend one part of the year merely 'inland' and another part 'on the coast'; they followed exactly the same sequence of movements, and occupied the same series of campsites, year in and year out. It was only during lean winter months that the direction and frequency of travel might vary from one year to the next. Otherwise, their annual cycle of movement took them literally in a circle: in early spring they went west to the coast, then south and east along the coast, and finally north up the river back to their starting point. Across the sound from the modern town of Kotzebue stands a mountain the Eskimos call Ingitqalik; old *Napaaqturmiut* people say that their parents spent their entire lives just travelling round and round that mountain.

The major means of summer transport for the *Napaaqturmiut*, as for most

Umiaks varied only slightly in design from one end of the Eskimo world to the other. Made of a wooden frame covered with a seal or walrus skin tarpaulin, a 9-metre (30-foot) long craft could easily carry a load of 900 kg (2000 lb) and eight passengers, yet be light enough when empty to be carried by four men. This model frame, from West Greenland, is made from bone and sinew.

other Eskimo groups, was the umiak, which was an open boat constructed of a wooden frame and waterproof cover made from the skins of several large seals or walruses. Umiaks were powered by a combination of paddles, oars and square-rigged sails. In much of Alaska, dogs were hitched to the boat by means of a long line. They trotted along the beach or river bank and tracked the vessel, which was kept away from shore by the helmsman and one person wielding an oar. When rounding a promontory, or when travelling to an island, the dogs were put inside the boat, and it proceeded under sail when travelling downwind, and by paddle otherwise.

The other Eskimo boat in widespread use, the kayak, was primarily a hunting craft. It was a slender vessel about six metres (nearly twenty feet) long and one metre (over three feet) wide, although the size and shape varied from one region to another. Like the umiak, the kayak was constructed of a wooden frame

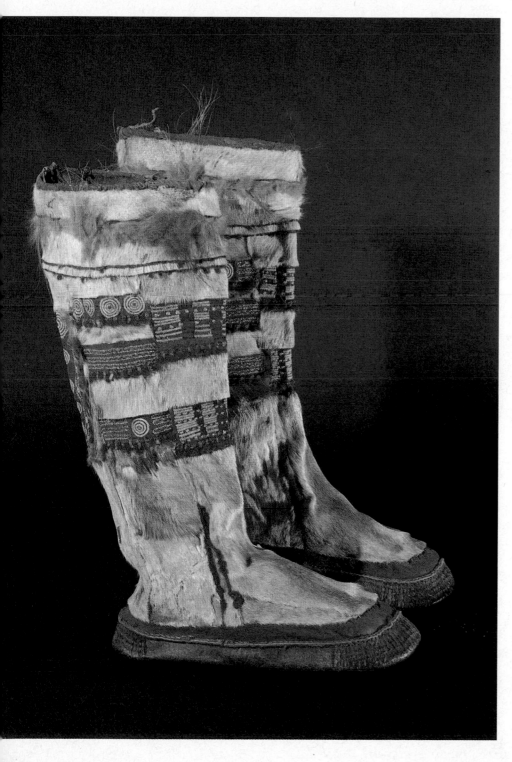

Footgear took a variety of forms according to season, purpose, raw material and the sex of the wearer. Aleuts and some Pacific Eskimo groups often went barefoot, whereas other Alaskan groups made a dozen or more distinctly different types of boot. The Alaskan boots seen here are of the fancy dress kind worn by men on special occasions. They are made of bearded sealskin bottoms and imported Siberian reindeer-skin uppers, decorated with strips of coloured seal and caribou skin, seal intestine, dyed dog hair, wolverine fur and coloured thread.

Kayak designs varied in detail from one region to another, but the basic plan of a slender, very fast hunting boat propelled by paddles never varied. This 150-year-old West Greenlandic model, seen resting on a pan of sea ice, shows the streamlined grace characteristic of the local style at the time. Projecting upward from the coaming is a round sealskin 'vest' that the hunter could pull up over his body to keep water from splashing into the hull. This particular craft was built small enough for a boy of about seven to ten years to use so that he could acquire the skills necessary to be a successful hunter.

85

In traditional times few families had more than two or three dogs, each of which was attached directly to the sled by a separate line. When there was much of a load, people had to assist the dogs by pulling and pushing. This small sled is from East Greenland, where the wood supply was very meagre.

covered with skin, but it was completely enclosed except for a small opening, or hatch – often two of them among the Aleuts – for the hunter. In some districts of Alaska the kayak was replaced by a small, skin- or bark-covered boat similar to an American Indian canoe in construction.

In regions where Eskimos lacked umiaks because of insufficient wood to build them, rafts made of several kayaks lashed together were used to transport people and equipment between islands and the mainland, and occasionally for longer journeys as well. In the Aleutian Islands, the rafting technique was employed primarily as a safety measure. When an unexpected storm caught several hunters out at sea in the same area, they lashed their boats together. The resulting craft was stable enough to keep from capsizing, yet flexible enough to bend in the waves and thus not be broken apart. In the Central Arctic, men walking inland with their families for the caribou-hunting season carried their kayaks on their shoulders, each boat upside down, with its owner's head inserted in the hatch. When the party came to a lake or river that was too deep to ford, two or three kayaks were lashed together to transport the people and their belongings across.

Winter was the best time for overland travel everywhere in the north. It was also the best time for any type of travel in regions where umiak transport was either unavailable or difficult, because sleds could be used to haul people and goods from place to place. Eskimo sleds varied in size and shape from one region to another. Wherever possible they were pulled by dogs, but since most families could not afford to keep a full team of eight or more dogs – three or four seems to have been the traditional norm in most regions – people often had to assist them. Poor families had no dogs at all and had to pull the sleds themselves; but that was still better than packing their belongings on their backs.

In parts of Southwest Alaska breast yokes were used to help in carrying heavy packs. A cord was affixed to one end, passed around the load and looped over the other end; the yoke itself was placed across the bearer's chest. This handsome model features a woman's face carved in relief and inset caribou teeth. These features served as charms to protect the traveller from harm.

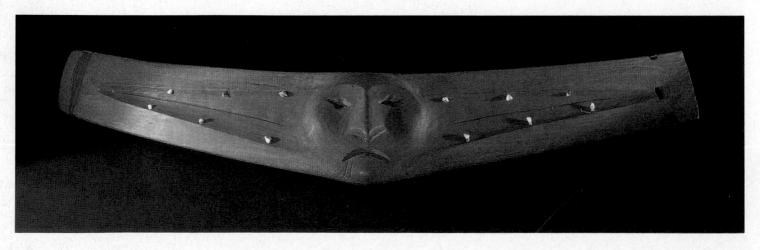

Traditional Eskimo dogs, which came in a wide range of sizes and colours, not only helped pull sleds in winter, they carried packs on their backs in summer, and, in the Western Arctic, were used to track umiaks. They were also used in hunting in some areas. They helped locate seal-breathing holes, for example, and haul the harvest back to camp. In some regions, they were used to bring to bay certain species of large game, such as musk-oxen and polar bears, by being released from the sled to overtake and harass the prey until their master caught up to make the kill. Occasionally dogs were used to bring down wounded caribou. Still another service performed by dogs was guard duty. They tended to stay near the houses of their owners, and were usually the first to signal the approach of strangers. Finally, dogs served as food. When all other resources failed, and people were beginning to cook and eat their own clothing, they would kill a dog and eat it instead. Among the Pacific and some Southwest Alaskan Eskimos, in fact, dogs were raised more as sources of meat than as beasts of burden.

Many Eskimo groups had to make at least one major move each year on foot. In the Central Arctic, people had to walk from their spring seal-hunting stations, on the coast, to their summer caribou-hunting grounds, some thirty to a hundred kilometres (twenty to sixty-five miles) or more inland. Later, they would have to carry the results of the hunt back out to the coast, or else return to the coast to retrieve supplies cached there the previous spring. The people in some of these groups, the Caribou Eskimos in particular, were splendid walkers. To them, a 150-kilometre (95-mile) trek with full equipment was not a particular burden, it was simply a normal part of life.

When travelling on foot, Eskimos carried their possessions in large bundles held on the back by straps across the chest and forehead. Infants were carried above the pack in the back of their mother's parka; everyone else had to walk. Each person who could carried something. Even the dogs bore large loads held in bags slung over their backs. Thus equipped, people and dogs walked slowly but steadily toward their destination. If they had too many goods to carry at one time, they cached those that were not absolutely necessary and returned for them later, by sled or by boat, if possible. Or they might transport their belongings in relays, moving a portion forward in the morning, and returning for the balance in the afternoon. They would have to discard whatever they could neither carry nor return for. Groups who had thus to travel on foot were among the poorest in the entire Eskimo world.

Glaciers and steep slopes covered by wind-packed snow offer precarious footing. In regions where this was a special problem Eskimos sometimes made bone crampons to lash to their boots to improve traction.

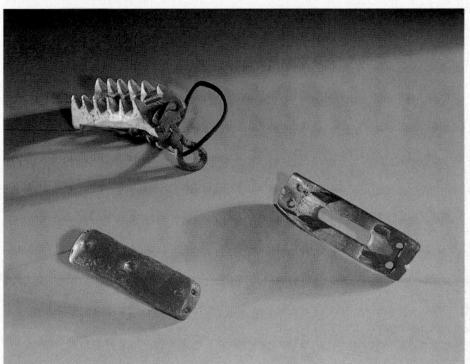

WORLD VIEW

To Eskimos, the universe possessed a fundamental unity in which several distinctions basic to the Western way of seeing things did not exist. Contrasts such as life and death, dreams and reality, and beginning and end had no meaning. Extremes of time, space and existence were all seen as different points on a continuum, or as different phases or aspects of a single, unified whole, which was reality. Eskimos did not even distinguish between the possible and the impossible; under the right conditions, *anything* was possible.

The Eskimos believed that every thing is imbued with a soul, or energy source, which conveys to its shape the potential for action, and a disposition, which determines its attitude toward other phenomena. A rock outcrop on a hillside, for example, is not an inherently lifeless feature of the landscape, but a vital being. Some outcrops kill any passer-by who has the temerity to approach them too closely. Others are actually people or animals whose bodies were transformed into rock by a shaman or spirit, there to stand transfixed until released by another powerful force. An outcrop is more than just rock because an animating force resides within it. When an Eskimo gazed out across the countryside, he did not see a static arrangement of land forms, as we would. He perceived a complex, exciting, and often frightening world of natural and supernatural phenomena in which even inert topographic features contained within them the potential for dynamic action.

Animate beings are also characterized by breath, in addition to a soul, a shape and a disposition. While this is not the force which gives them life – the soul does that – breath gives to animals and people their special ability to interact with the Spirit of the Air, and this means they have more power than plants and rocks do.

Human beings, in addition to the four fundamental characteristics mentioned so far, also have *names*. To most Eskimos, a name possessed its own power, as well as, or apart from, that conveyed by a soul, a disposition and breath. This is why people, who have all of these qualities, are generally more powerful than seals, or rocks, or caribou. Names were much more than mere labels, they were sacred.

An infant was not considered human until it had been named. The assignment of a name to a newborn baby was therefore an urgent matter. An infant was not regarded as a unique individual, but as the fresh embodiment of a dead person's soul. All that was required to complete the reincarnation process was to assign to the baby a deceased person's name.

After proper magical preparations, shamans were able to see into the bodies of others, and to expose their own internal anatomy to view. These powers are symbolized in this nineteenth-century mask from the Lower Kuskokwim River, Alaska.

Above: Most of the spirits inhabiting the Eskimo world were hostile to humans, and had to be placated or cajoled into allowing people to live in peace and comfort. Given this view, it is not surprising that most material representations of spirits had a decidedly sinister appearance, such as this wood figure with inlaid teeth from northern Alaska.

Right: Many masks represented the spirits of animals or supernatural beings. When an actor in a festival put on such a mask he became imbued with the spirit being represented. This complex mask from southwestern Alaska evidently represents a supernatural creature, but the symbolism intended by its various components has not been recorded.

The inventory of names available to the members of an Eskimo society was by no means fixed. Most people ended up with several names before they died, and the same name could be held by several individuals at the same time. In declining populations, such as those suffering from a series of famines, the supply of names sometimes exceeded the number of people available to receive them. Growing populations, on the other hand, had to invent new ones in order to satisfy the increased demand, although shamanistic intercession often was necessary for this to occur. In these, as in most matters, Eskimos were not doctrinaire practitioners of a systematically elaborated conception of reality, but rather flexible interpreters of a world view that contained what Westerners would regard as many inconsistencies and loose ends.

Given the importance they attached to names, Eskimos in some regions were remarkably casual about bestowing them. They did not attempt to discover whose soul might have reappeared in infant form and then name the baby accordingly, nor did they care whether or not more than one child was named after the same person. In some regions, babies were automatically named after the most recently deceased person. Since most groups did not differentiate between male and female appellations, this procedure was not as awkward as it seems. In other regions the name of almost any deceased person would do, selection apparently being based more on the whim of one of the parents or grandparents than on any serious consideration of the consequences.

In Southwest Alaska, however, name-giving and name use were treated much more carefully. Name-givers and shamans were usually involved, and the bestowal of a name was an occasion for ceremony. Once a name had been given, it could no longer be uttered, because real names were considered too sacred for everyday use. People had to use nicknames and circumlocutions to address and refer to one another.

Asiatic Eskimos attempted to discover whose soul was involved even before a baby was delivered. They analysed dreams and pondered events, seeking clues as to who was about to be reborn. If they had not identified the person by the time the infant arrived, its physical features were scrutinized for resemblances to a deceased person. If a child died after a name had been assigned, people concluded that they had given it the wrong one. If it merely became sick, they assumed that more names were needed, and kept adding them until the infant's health improved.

In East Greenland a child was given several names. Some of them were those of deceased persons, but many were words for objects drawn from the general vocabulary of the language: a lamp, perhaps, or a kind of rock. After a person died it was forbidden to mention even one of his names or else his soul would return to haunt the one who uttered it. This was no problem in the case of words that were names and nothing else, but it meant that names taken from objects could no longer be used to refer to those objects. New words had to be invented. When another child was born it might receive some of the tabooed names, which could then be spoken once again, but the corresponding objects kept the new appellations which had been assigned to them. By accumulation over the years, this custom led to changes in whole sections of the East Greenlandic vocabulary.

Once a name had been bestowed, it became a compelling factor in the development of a child's character and personality, and a crucial element in his or her relations with other people. Many early observers of Eskimos commented on how spoiled the children seemed to be. They could do almost anything they wanted without fear of punishment. Outsiders who stayed long enough to learn the Eskimo language were further surprised to hear a child addressed as 'mother' or 'grandfather' by its own parents, and by corresponding but equally incongruous terms, such as 'aunt' or 'cousin', by everyone else. Eventually they learned that the child in question had been named after someone who had been

related to the members of the group in the precise way suggested by the various kinship terms. A responsible Eskimo father did not want to spoil his young son, but he shrank from the idea of chastising his grandmother, even if she had now moved into the body of his son.

Death was simply the release from a body of the breath, disposition, soul and name. The body would decay, and in time disappear, but the other, important qualities of a person would endure. They would survive somewhere until reincarnated in another human form. The recycling of souls, names and dispositions through a succession of bodies was thought to continue forever. The idea of being reborn did not bother Eskimos for they knew that they would always reappear in human form rather than, say, as animals. Furthermore, although they deplored the suffering associated with hunger, cold or injury, they rejoiced in most other aspects of their humanity. The idea of transcending the life and death cycle would have had no appeal to them at all.

Eskimos were very attentive to the needs of the newly released soul, for a disaffected soul could cause extraordinary suffering among the people it left behind. To please a soul, various things a person had used in life would be placed on his or her grave, or near the body. A woman would be buried with her needles, lamp, pots and other utensils, while a man would have his tools and weapons laid beside his body. Important or scarce items, such as boats or lamps, might be reproduced in miniature for use as grave goods. As long as objects were represented in some way, their souls would accompany that of the deceased, which thus would have a comfortable existence until re-embodied in the form of a new baby.

The treatment of the body varied considerably from one region to another. Among most Eastern Eskimo groups, bodies and the associated grave goods were placed at some convenient spot on the ground and covered with rocks, if possible, or simply left in the snow, if not. In parts of Northwest Alaska bodies were buried in the ground, while in others they were placed in a flexed position in wooden coffins, along with the grave goods, and set on scaffolds. Burials were isolated in some areas, and placed in graveyards in others. Some Southwest Alaskan groups buried their dead underground or on scaffolds in cemeteries notable for numerous wooden monuments, effigies and elaborately displayed grave goods and other ritual paraphernalia. Asiatic Eskimos ritually dismembered the bodies of the deceased prior to burial, and some Aleut groups mummified their dead and placed them in caves.

The souls of departed human beings entered a spirit world that was a large and complex domain. It contained not only the souls of people, animals and other objects, but also an assortment of creatures from the realm of both ordinary and extraordinary experience. Included were birds, fish, and other animals of ordinary shape but of extraordinary size; dragons; creatures exactly like people but only a few inches high; mermaids; and monstrous creatures of distorted human or animal form. Some of them were sinister, some were harmless, and some were even humorous or pleasant. But they were all *there*, and most of them could be seen by human beings whenever they chose to let themselves become visible. At a somewhat more remote level were several spirits which lacked physical shape, although many of them could acquire one, usually of their own choosing, for a brief period of time. At the most remote level of all were from one to three spirits that were fundamentally more mysterious and powerful than all the others.

The major spirit in the Eskimo pantheon in most regions was the Spirit of the Air. This was the mystic power that permeated the entire world and the atmosphere around it. Its force was felt through the wind and weather, which influenced everything in nature, and it was thus the most powerful phenomenon in the universe. The Netsilik Eskimos believed that one manifestation of the Spirit of the Air was the Storm Spirit, whom they called Naartsuk.

Eskimos characteristically combined practical, artistic, religious and other qualities in single objects. Indeed, it never occurred to them that an item should be specialized in these respects, their technology thus reflecting the unity of their life in general. This tendency is illustrated here by two items from Southwest Alaska.

Left: Natural and supernatural beings were believed to be able to communicate directly with one another. On the bottom of this handsome bentwood serving dish we see a bull caribou (on the right) linked to its spiritual counterpart, which is identified as such by its bizarre appendages.

Right: This storage box carved from a single block of wood represents a seal lying on its back, with its spirit represented by a human-like face on the detachable lid. The eyes and mouth are represented by pieces of inlaid ivory, and the wrists of the flippers are crossed by ivory bars.

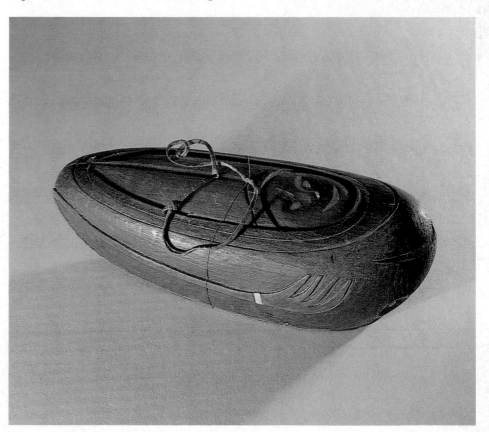

Right: The world was believed to be filled with spirits, some of which were friendly to people, but most of which were hostile. One common way to represent the latter in the dance festivals of Southwest Alaska was through masks such as this, with its distorted, semi-human face. Much of the knowledge of the extensive symbolism involved in the form and painting of these masks unfortunately has been lost.

Left: In Southwest Alaska grave goods were supplemented by wooden effigies intended to placate the souls of the deceased. They were not worn, but placed on posts near the grave. Normally they were erected as memorials during the first Feast of the Dead to occur after the person died. This example, which probably dates from the nineteenth century, originally had inlaid ivory eyes and mouth, but the latter was lost.

Naartsuk was originally the child of a giant and his wife, both of whom were murdered, first the father, then the mother. The murderers left the child to its fate, close to the spot where the parents had been killed. This evildoing turned the child into a spirit, which flew up into the sky and became the lord of the weather. It is always dressed in a full costume of caribou skin – a dress with tunic and breeches made in one piece, and very wide, as worn by children generally. When Naartsuk shakes his dress, air rushes out from all the loose spaces in his clothing, and the winds begin to flow.
(Knud Rasmussen. *Intellectual Culture of the Iglulik Eskimos. Report of the Fifth Thule Expedition 1921–24, Vol. VII, No. 1, p. 72, 1929.*)

The second most influential spirit, in most regions, was the Spirit of the Sea. It controlled the spirits, and thus, by extension, the souls of all the creatures living in the ocean. Since most Eskimo groups depended upon sea mammals for their survival, its influence on their lives was considerable. (In parts of Southwest Alaska, in place of the Spirit of the Sea, there was a Master of each species living under the sea.)

The Spirit of the Moon was the final member of the Eskimo trinity, although apparently it was not recognized as such in all regions. It was associated with the moon, but was not the moon itself. The Moon Spirit was thought to have great influence over land animals, hence was of special importance to groups highly dependent on caribou.

These three spirits ultimately controlled practically everything in the Eskimo environment. They could either exercise their power directly, or else delegate to the myriad lesser spirits the power to act more or less independently. Their influence over people was exercised indirectly through the granting or withholding of good weather and abundant game supplies. The Eskimos feared these spirits but did not worship them; rather they attempted to placate the spirits and persuade them to be munificent. To achieve this, they had to obey an extraordinary number of rules, or taboos, which experience or shamanistic insight had suggested would please or pacify both the major spirits and the souls of the animals the hunters intended to kill.

The fact that animals had souls was profoundly troubling to responsible Eskimo hunters. As an Iglulik man expressed it to Knud Rasmussen:

> The greatest peril of life lies in the fact that human food consists entirely of souls. All the creatures that we have to kill and eat, all those that we have to strike down and destroy to make clothes for ourselves, have souls, like we have, souls that do not perish with the body, and which therefore must be propitiated lest they should revenge themselves on us for taking away their bodies.
> (*Intellectual Culture of the Iglulik Eskimos, Vol. VII, No. I*, p. 56, 1929.)

If all the taboos were obeyed, animals allowed themselves to be killed, and good health and prosperity descended upon the hunter and his family. If some were broken, no matter how innocently, famine or accident or sickness was certain to follow. There were so many taboos, however, that no one even knew them all, much less remembered them at the appropriate times. Consequently,

Below: Eskimos believed that game was not 'taken' by a hunter, but permitted itself to be killed. People thus went to great lengths to please the spirits of the animals they depended on for their own survival. This wooden effigy of a bowhead whale, when lashed to a boat and ritually imbued with magical power by a shaman, pleased the whales' souls and greatly enhanced the hunters' chance of success.

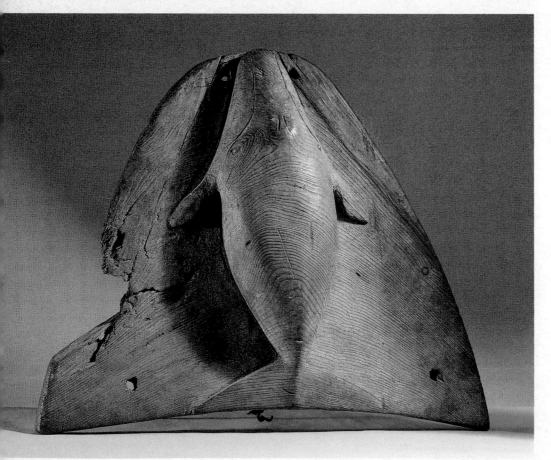

mishaps of one kind or another were always befalling people.

The number of taboos that had to be followed was enormous. Here, for instance, are the ones that the inhabitants of a Copper Eskimo settlement had to take into account to ensure success in seal hunting. First, there were several taboos which applied all the time. Things of land and sea could never be brought into contact, which meant that sea-mammal meat and land-mammal meat could never be placed in the same pot. In addition, seal sinew could never be used for sewing, cod could never be eaten with blubber stored in sealskin bags since the previous spring, and fresh caribou meat could never be placed on a platform together with seal meat or charr.

Other taboos varied to some extent according to season and location, so let us assume that it was early January, that the village of snow houses was situated several kilometres out on the solidly frozen sea, and that the sun had not yet risen from its several-week-long stay below the horizon. Under these conditions,

Right: The face on this mask from western Alaska represents the spirit of the moon. The board around the face symbolizes air, and the hoops around the board signify levels of the cosmos. The feathers represent stars. In many regions the Spirits of the Air and the Moon were major deities; different groups of stars represented a variety of creatures and mythical beings.

Left: The spirits of major game animals were placated in festivals and with charms. This box, which was used to store whale lance blades, was carved in the shape of a whale, and thus served as a charm as well as a container. Blades kept in such a box were believed to be particularly effective in dispatching a wounded whale.

the following taboos applied with specific reference to seal-hunting success: (1) caribou meat and charr could not be cooked at all, but had to be eaten raw; (2) caribou skins could not be sewn at all; (3) no sewing of any kind could be done by a hunter's wife on the day of a successful hunt; (4) a seal carcass had to have water dripped into its mouth as an offering as soon as it was brought into the house; (5) a whole series of prohibitions against scraping hoar frost off the window were in effect; (6) as long as an unbutchered seal was in the house, the bed cover could not be shaken out over the floor, no one could rearrange the plaited willow twig mat that lay on the bed, no oil could drip on the floor, and no work could be done in wood or stone.

Besides the many taboos which pertained to certain seasons and locations, there were others which applied to specific events in a person's life cycle. For example, when a Copper Eskimo boy killed his first seal, his mother had to go

Ravens, intelligent, mischevious birds that often lurk around the fringes of settlements, were regarded by Eskimos with a mixture of amusement and awe. The ambivalence carried over into folklore and ritual, in which the birds played prominent roles. This stylized mask represents Raven, the spirit of the raven species, and is an example of a rather common form in Southwest Alaska.

through a ritual performance of pretending to weep and to wrestle with him for possession of the carcass. When the carcass was finally brought into the house, it had to be left untouched for several hours. After the appropriate length of time had elapsed, the mother tied her belt around the seal's head, reserving that part for herself, and the rest of the women in the village hacked apart the rest of it, each trying to obtain for herself the largest piece. Birth or death were occasions for many additional taboos, as was an illness, or a woman's menstrual period, particularly her first.

Taboos were so numerous that they formed a sort of straitjacket around all a person's inclinations and movements. There was hardly a moment when an Eskimo could feel master of himself. Many people sought ways to circumvent the laws which so restricted their freedom of action. A Copper Eskimo wife who had to mend some clothes might give them to her mother or to some other woman whose husband was not hunting that day. In Northwest Alaska an

Upper Kobuk girl who in her own country would have to undergo an entire year of privation upon her first menstruation might be sent to live with relatives in another country where the menarche taboos were less severe. Or people might just ignore a taboo in hopes that it had lapsed, or that it might not be enforced on a given occasion. Evading or ignoring taboos exposed one to grave risk, however, since, while the manoeuvre might work, it might also end in disaster.

People were not entirely at the mercy of the spirit world, however. One resource they had was the charm, a small object whose associated spirit would use its power to improve the owner's hunting success, to defend him against hostile spirits, or to help in some other precise way. Since the need for spiritual assistance or protection was continuous and all-pervasive, Eskimos tried to collect a large number of charms, each of which would perform a specific helpful function.

The number and variety of objects which served as charms is remarkable. A ptarmigan's claw, a dried ermine skin, a piece of root, an ivory carving, a piece of stone, a raven's beak, a piece of wood, a dried flower – all were employed for the purpose. Personal charms normally were carried somewhere on the body. They could be attached to one's belt, sewn on the clothing, hung by a string around the neck, or carried in a pouch. Most people owned several, and a few owned literally dozens – all of which they had to carry about at all times. Others were incorporated into weapons or tools, usually as carved handles or other components. Family charms were placed at some appropriate location inside or just

A drag float was made from the skin of an entire seal which was removed and modified in such a way as to make it resemble a large balloon. It was inflated by blowing through a mouthpiece permanently attached at one end and capped with a plug. The plugs were often carved to resemble human or animal faces, serving also as charms to ensure future success in hunting. The one shown here was carved from ivory into the form of a human face, with inlaid bead eyes and another bead in its mouth. It also has tattoo marks inscribed on the chin, suggesting that it represents a female.

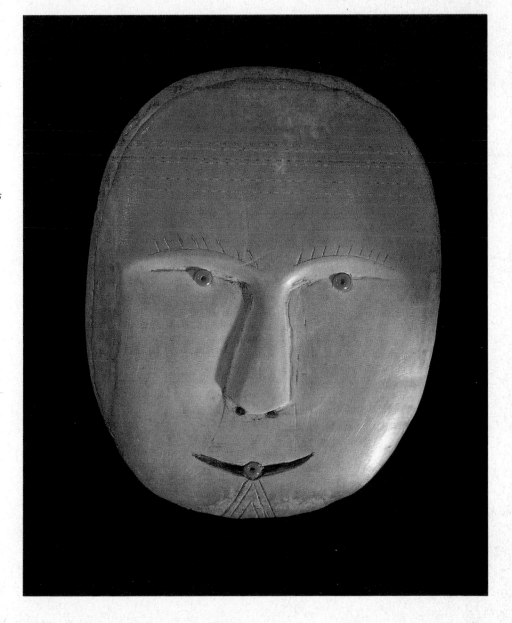

outside the house, depending on the specific purpose of the charm concerned.

The power of such an otherwise inconsequential object was usually ascertained by a shaman, who then either sold or gave it to its subsequent owner. Alternatively, awareness of an object's potential as a charm might come to one spontaneously in a dream, or a coincidence might suggest that a particular object would function effectively as a charm. If a man happened to have extraordinary seal-hunting success one day, and upon his return home found a gull feather in the bottom of his kayak, he might infer that the feather was the source of his good fortune. He would keep it in the kayak, carefully hidden and protected. If further experience confirmed his initial impression, the feather acquired the status of a charm.

Once acquired, a charm would be passed from generation to generation, either along family lines or, in Asia and Southwest Alaska, along lineage or clan lines. The natural tendency for their number to increase over time was offset by the fact that some either lost their power, or failed to exercise it for a particular owner. Ineffective charms were discarded. Others might decay, break, or be lost, so that the total number of charms in use at any one time probably remained more or less constant.

Another source of supernatural power was the spell. A spell is a word, or a series of words – spoken in some cases, sung in others – which produces a specific magical effect, such as killing a wounded whale, moderating a severe windstorm, or defending a person from the attacks of ghosts. In most cases the words themselves seem to have been meaningless. Their power inhered not in their semantic substance but in their form.

A spell usually originated with a shaman, and an ordinary person would purchase it. Sometimes, however, a layman might hear words uttered by a spirit while he was hunting, and later learn in a dream how to use them as a spell. Once acquired, a spell could be sold or given as a legacy, but a spell, like a charm, normally was effective only for its legitimate owner. Just in case it might work for someone else, however, the owner did not want a spell to become known to anyone except a purchaser or a chosen beneficiary. Its power would decline with over-use, so even its possessor would employ it selectively. Owners of particularly powerful spells might use them only once or twice in their entire lives, usually in extreme situations where the survival of a hunting crew or settlement was at stake.

More important even than the charm or the spell was the shaman. A shaman was an otherwise unexceptional person, a man or a woman, who had an extraordinary ability to communicate with and to influence the actions of spirits. The power stemmed from the person's ability to dissociate his own soul from his body, and thus to deal with spirits on their own terms. The shaman's spirit became associated with one or more lesser spirits, known as 'familiars', who became his servants. They would advise and protect him, investigate problems, and otherwise assist him in performing shamanistic duties.

Every Eskimo had some ability to deal directly with the spirit world. The power of shamans was simply much greater in this respect than that of anyone else, and shamans differed among themselves in ability as well. Just how they acquired their power varied from one region to another. In some regions, it simply devolved upon them spontaneously. In most, however, a person had to seek power deliberately, either through apprenticeship to a practising shaman, or through some sort of mystical experience, which might come about as a result of fasting on a mountain top or in a cave for an extended period. Through

Each shaman was associated with one or more special spirits, or 'familiars', on whom they relied for help in curing, divining, and communicating with other spirits. This wooden figurine represents the familiar spirit of a nineteenth-century East Greenlandic shaman named Taqhisima.

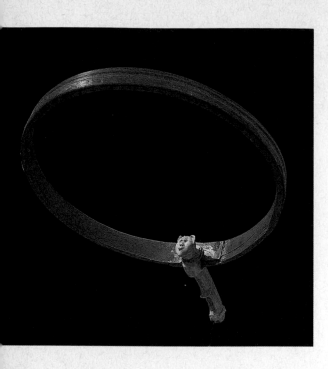

Above: The ivory handle of this drum frame is apparently an effigy of one of a shaman's familiar spirits. Drums were indispensable items during shamanistic performances, as well as during occasions of a less serious nature.

Right: The meaning of this complex mask has not been recorded. It apparently represents a shaman's spirit flight, with the face in the centre of the body representing the shaman's soul.

whichever process happened to work in his particular country, a shaman acquired the ability temporarily to free his soul from his body, and through the soul to establish a direct bond with the spirits who were to become his familiars.

The most important services performed by shamans were to discover the cause of a calamity, such as a sickness, injury, flood or famine, and to prescribe a cure. Since most troubles were caused by offended spirits, the diagnosis typically involved determining which spirit had been insulted and why. Usually it was discovered that some group or individual had broken a taboo and had not confessed the transgression to anyone else. The cure required the performance of a ritual or, more often, adherence to one or more special taboos – in addition to all the regular ones – by the offending party.

The very best shamans could do much more than diagnose problems and prescribe solutions. They could also produce success in hunting, forecast and sometimes change the weather, foretell the future, see what was happening far away, produce charms and spells, communicate with the souls of the dead, and perform miracles of various kinds. Two examples of actual cases from the late nineteenth century illustrate both the kinds of things that shamans could do and their typical mode of operation.

The first concerns a Northwest Alaskan family who spent most of the year in the Kivalina region, but who went to Point Hope each spring for whaling. One year they were apprehensive about making the trip because there had been a great deal of European disease at Point Hope recently and many people had died from it. So they hired a shaman named Aivinguaq to study the situation and tell them what to do.

Aivinguaq gathered everyone together in a darkened house. After they were seated, he removed from his kit a miniature tent made of the intestines of a bearded seal, a doll, and a tiny lamp. He placed the doll and lamp inside the tent, shut the flap, and began to sing and beat his drum. After a while a light went on inside the tent, and the doll stood up and began to walk around; those in the audience could see its moving shadow on the tent's translucent walls. A dialogue between Aivinguaq and the doll, held in an incomprehensible language, ensued. After a few minutes' conversation, the doll lay down again, the light in the little tent went out, and the shaman resumed his drumming and singing. After he had finished his song and had returned the paraphernalia to his bag, Aivinguaq announced that it was fine to go to Point Hope: no member of the family would get sick that year. Furthermore, the crew to which they belonged would take three whales, an extraordinary number for a single crew in one season. So the family followed his recommendations, and everything came to pass as he predicted.

The second example is also from Northwest Alaska, this time from the Lower Noatak region. The shaman concerned, whose name was Ikinyiq, was performing partly for his own pleasure, and partly to impress the people in the settlement with his ability. After gathering everyone together in the darkened house and instructing them to be silent, he clothed himself in heavy winter garments. A prolonged period of singing and drumming was followed by a sudden brief silence which was succeeded by a whooshing sound and a rattling of the skylight. Then more silence. Ikinyiq stood still in the middle of the floor. After an hour or so of complete silence and immobility, the skylight rattled again, there was another whooshing sound, and Ikinyiq's motionless body suddenly became animated. After another period of drumming and singing, he described to the audience what had happened.

Ikinyiq told them that he – that is, his soul – had just made a visit to the moon. The movement of the soul through the skylight was what had made the peculiar sounds as it left and re-entered the house. While on the moon, it had encountered the souls of two Point Hope shamans. So Ikinyiq was able to tell his audience what the earth looked like from the moon, and also provide them with the latest news from Point Hope.

Later that spring, some Lower Noatak families went to Point Hope for the whaling season. Just after they arrived they encountered one of the two shamans Ikinyiq claimed to have seen during his visit to the moon. The shaman's immediate reaction upon seeing them was to inquire about his Noatak counterpart who, he said, he had recently met on the moon. This astounded the Noatakers, at least some of whom had been sceptical of Ikinyiq's claims. They also discovered that everything Ikinyiq had told them about events in Point Hope was true. He could not have learned about those events in any other way because no other Noatakers and Point Hopers had been in contact since the previous summer.

The use of magic songs was a common way for shamans to generate the force required to perform extraordinary feats. It was also considered helpful to have an audience, and sometimes to have an apprentice helper. Although most shamans acquired their magical powers in solitude, they usually exercised them in public. If they did not, they would be suspected of performing black magic, a crime punishable by death. The animation of the doll and the spirit flight, while beyond the capacity of the ordinary person, were both commonplace examples of shamanistic endeavour. Other techniques included trance, temporary

Aleuts and Southwest Alaskan Eskimos wore bentwood visors when hunting in kayaks. These hats served both to reduce glare and to transport a variety of charms to help increase the chances of a successful hunt and a safe return. They possibly also bore symbols of the wearer's status. The meanings of the several components of this specific visor unfortunately were not recorded.

possession of the shaman's body by another spirit, and divination through certain mechanical procedures and the analysis of signs and portents.

Shamans were by no means uniformly successful in practising their trade. Occasionally one would prepare an elaborate seance or other dramatic feat and fail completely to achieve what he had promised. Eskimos, who had a keen sense of the absurd, would ordinarily regard this as hilarious, particularly if the shaman had boasted of his prowess. His failure, and his embarrassed attempts to explain it away, would be greeted with a great deal of laughter and cynical commentary. Unless such a shaman promptly produced more successful results, his reputation would be destroyed, and his career would be at an end.

Being ordinary human beings in most respects, shamans were not immune to corruption or altogether free from the baser human tendencies, and some abused their power. A few were sorcerers, and others became involved in power struggles with competitors. As sorcerers, they typically tried to bring harm or even death to certain individuals. In power struggles, they frequently brought disaster to families or even to entire societies in their efforts to defeat one another. Most of the worst famines in recorded Eskimo history have been explained by the survivors as the consequences of shamanistic conflict. A shaman who was causing harm to people, be it deliberately, more or less by default through a power struggle, or through outright incompetence, was a threat to his fellow man, and he would be shunned or killed unless he changed his ways.

The majority of shamans used their special knowledge of and relationship with the spirit world for the benefit of the community to which they belonged. Eskimos needed to have shamans who were successful. The inability of a braggart to fly to the moon or to turn himself into a mouse would be funny, but the failure of a mature shaman to ascertain the cause of a famine would be a disaster. Without shamans, life would have been difficult indeed.

Shamans also played central roles in the festivals that were held from time to time. Among the Eastern Eskimos, festivals tended to be held whenever and wherever an aggregation of people and the accumulation of a large stock of food provided both the opportunity and means to have one. These festivals, being spontaneous in nature, required little special preparation, and were relatively free of ritual practices not directly associated with taboos. People danced, sang, feasted, played games, traded, gossiped and slept, pretty much as they wanted to. However, shamans characteristically seized the opportunity that such gatherings offered to display their powers, even if their performances were not an essential part of the festival itself.

Western Eskimos held similarly casual gatherings, but they also engaged in a regular series of formal festivals many of which had distinct religious overtones. Although the festival calendar was determined largely by tradition, shamans were the people who interpreted that tradition. They played an important part in the planning of specific events, and they usually held a central position in the festivals themselves.

The most elaborate festivals known from any part of the Eskimo world took place in the large whaling villages of Northwest Alaska, and in Southwest Alaska generally. No doubt the Aleuts and Pacific Eskimos had similarly or even more complex festival calendars, but the depredations of the Russians brought them to such an early halt that we know very little about them.

The elaborate development of festivals in the Western Arctic can be illustrated by the *Ungalaqlingmiut*, who lived along the West Alaskan coast. These people celebrated one cycle of festivals according to a precise seasonal calendar, and another series of more lavish events on an intermittent basis.

The regular festival season began in mid- to late November with the two-day Asking Festival. On the first night men and older boys paraded through the village, their faces blackened with charcoal and oil, their naked bodies painted with stripes and dots. They toured single file through' the houses, each carrying a

A shaman could release his spirit from his body and, in spirit form, fly to other parts of the world or into the cosmos. There he observed conditions or consulted with other spirits, subsequently returning with his information. This figurine from Point Hope, Alaska, depicts a shaman in the midst of such a flight. It was made from whale vertebrae, walrus ivory, wood, seal hide and stone, and was probably used on ceremonial occasions.

dish for donations of food. When they returned to the 'kashim' the men washed, then sat down to feast on the food they had collected, sharing it with older men who had waited for them there. On the second night the men were again in the 'kashim' and the women were in the houses. A designated messenger, carrying a special wand, stood in the middle of the room. Any man could tell him the name of something he wanted to have, and the name of the woman from whom he wished to have it. The messenger then went to that woman's house and told her of the man's request. She then asked for something she wanted in return, and the wand-bearer conveyed her message to the man waiting in the 'kashim'. This process continued until everyone had asked for something. When the messenger finished, the men went home, collected the articles for which they had been asked, and returned to the 'kashim' for a dance. The women joined them there, bringing their gifts. The exchanges were made with the messenger acting as intermediary. At that time a man could ask the woman he had named, if she was unmarried, to sleep with him that night.

Approximately ten days after the conclusion of the Asking Festival the first Festival of the Dead was held. Whereas the primary purpose of the Asking Festival was the celebration and reinforcement of social solidarity among the inhabitants of the village, this event was to propitiate the souls of the recently deceased through offerings of food, water and clothing. It consisted of a series of ritual graveside observances by the members of the different families interspersed with communal songs, dances and other activities in the 'kashim'. As was always the case, the period in which this festival occurred was marked by the imposition of a large number of special taboos in addition to those ordinarily in effect.

The Bladder Festival, the major event in the festival calendar, began in mid-December and lasted for six days. It consisted of a long and complex series of rituals, dances, song presentations and feasts designed to ensure a successful seal hunt the following spring. The focus of the event was the seal bladder, wherein the soul of the seal was believed to reside. The inflated bladders of all of the seals that had been killed during the preceding year were brought forth and feasted

Masks were not just carvings, but symbolic manifestations of some spirit or quality which they represented in festivals, and with which their wearer was temporarily imbued. Their use was always accompanied by dance and song, all of which played some role in a larger story. This owl mask, for example, was worn during a complex dance celebrating the diversity and abundance of animals which, in turn, was part of the week-long Bladder Festival in southwestern Alaska.

and entertained during a series of ritual observances. On the last day they were returned to the sea through holes chopped in the ice so that the souls contained within them could be born once again as seals. Other seals who witnessed this act would be more willing to allow themselves to be killed in the future, knowing that their souls, too, eventually would be returned to their home in the sea.

Two days after the Bladder Festival was over, a second Festival of the Dead was held. The third was celebrated just before the start of the fishing season the following summer, concluding the regular annual festival cycle.

Altogether the *Ungalaqlingmiut* festivals occupied a minimum of twelve days each year, and took nearly twice that long to prepare for. From time to time, these regular festivals were supplemented by the Messenger Feast and the Great Festival of the Dead, both of which lasted six days or more and took years of systematic effort to prepare for. The Messenger Feast was held to celebrate good relations between the people of two different settlements or societies, while the Great Festival of the Dead, like its more modest annual counterpart, was performed to provide comfort to the souls of the dead. During a year in which one of these special events was held, almost a third of an adult's waking hours might be devoted to preparation for or participation in festivals.

Finger masks were made only in southwestern Alaska, where they were worn primarily by women during dance festivals. The face in the centre of this one apparently represents the Moon Spirit, a very important member of the pantheon. The wooden portion of the mask is trimmed with caribou hair.

EXPRESSION

The graceful form of this broken Thule Culture (c. AD 1000) ivory comb epitomizes the Eskimo penchant for infusing items of everyday use with artistic elegance. Most of the teeth have been broken off, but the stylized female figure and the incised decorations are still intact.

One day in May 1922, the Danish explorer Knud Rasmussen arrived at the Caribou Eskimo settlement of Nahiktartorvik, far out in the barren lands west of Hudson Bay. Its twenty-three inhabitants had experienced a winter of extreme privation which had only just been relieved by the arrival of the northward caribou migration. They were living in houses made of rapidly decaying snow-block walls roofed over with hastily made tarpaulins of raw caribou skin. Despite the season, snow still covered the ground. Shortly after Rasmussen's arrival, a violent storm struck. Rain, thunder and lightning, and gale force winds quickly transformed the camp into a morass of melting snow, mud and water. A more desolate and uncomfortable scene is difficult to imagine.

In the midst of the storm Rasmussen ventured out of his own relatively dry canvas tent to see how his neighbours were faring. He peeked through one of the many holes in the first house he came to and was astonished to hear its soaking occupants singing. Completely unmindful of the chaos around them, they thought only of their joy at having food again. Rasmussen staggered through the slush and mud to another house, and again peeked through a hole in the wall. This time he discovered the people inside completely absorbed in a game of cards – an activity they had learned from Hudson's Bay Company traders – laughing and exclaiming with pleasure. Rasmussen suddenly understood that people born to such hardship could not take discomfort seriously, and he realized that one of the key elements in the Eskimos' talent for survival in the north was their ability to react to difficult situations cheerfully.

Eskimos thought it important to be happy. A happy person was considered a capable person, a reliable person – in short, a good person; an unhappy one was thought to be deficient in some significant respect. Happiness was expressed through a pleasant demeanour, an open, smiling face, and animated conversation and gestures. Eskimos had a keen sense of humour, frequently ribald, and often tinged with irony. These characteristics led, no doubt, to the Western view of Eskimos as being a perpetually lighthearted, rather simple people.

Actually, of course, Eskimos were no strangers to anger, fear, anxiety, frustration, pain and sorrow, but the extent to which these sentiments were allowed to be *expressed* varied significantly. Pain was to be accepted stoically and not shown at all. Fear and anxiety could be expressed quietly by women, partly verbally and partly by a tense facial expression, but for men to exhibit such weakness was shameful. Sorrow, on the other hand, could be expressed openly by almost anyone, male or female, by crying.

Anti-social sentiments such as anger, greed and frustration were not supposed to receive overt expression at all. They emerged anyway, of course, but usually in the form of play. If a man were angry with his brother, he might express that fact in the guise of a word game by calling him a number of offensive names, or by describing him in harsh terms. His smiles and the extreme nature of his language would make his remarks seem like a joke. Actually, he would be expressing a genuine negative sentiment in the only way permitted in his society. At the same time, the brother's willingness to receive such abuse without losing his temper, or perhaps to respond to it in the same joking manner, was considered proof that the underlying bond between the two men was very strong. The remark that someone 'can call me any old name and I won't get mad' is a classic Eskimo way of identifying to others a close friend or favourite relative.

Truly intense sentiments of *any* kind had no structured form of expression. This was just as true of joy and grief as it was of hatred, emotions which were of course felt from time to time. When they were, they tended to be expressed in a violent manner, such as by suicide or physical assault, by loss of consciousness, or through generally bizarre behaviour, such as running around naked in the snow. Various forms of the last have been designated by Westerners as 'Arctic hysteria'.

Traditionally approved patterns of emotional expression were somewhat more varied among the Western than among the Eastern Eskimos. In the west, family heads and village chiefs were expected to maintain a certain dignity and reserve no matter what emotion they felt. In some areas, mothers- and sons-in-law were not supposed to look directly at or talk directly to each other – even if they were very fond of one another. Young married women were expected to smile pleasantly, talk quietly and generally maintain an unobtrusive presence in the community, whereas old ladies could laugh and talk and tease and joke and pour forth a torrent of abuse or commentary any time they pleased.

Eskimos sometimes guffawed or cackled when amused, but usually gently chuckled with the mouth open, a quiet 'heeeeee!'. One can still travel the whole way across the top of North America and hear this sound, but nothing quite like it anywhere else. Similarly widespread was the tendency to communicate with

Food was served in stone pots in the Eastern Arctic, and in wooden bowls or dishes in the West. This elegant serving dish was probably used during ceremonial feasts in southwestern Alaska. The handles are in the form of masked human heads. The basin is decorated with a mythological design, and the rim is enhanced with inlaid ivory beads. The precise meaning of these symbols was not recorded.

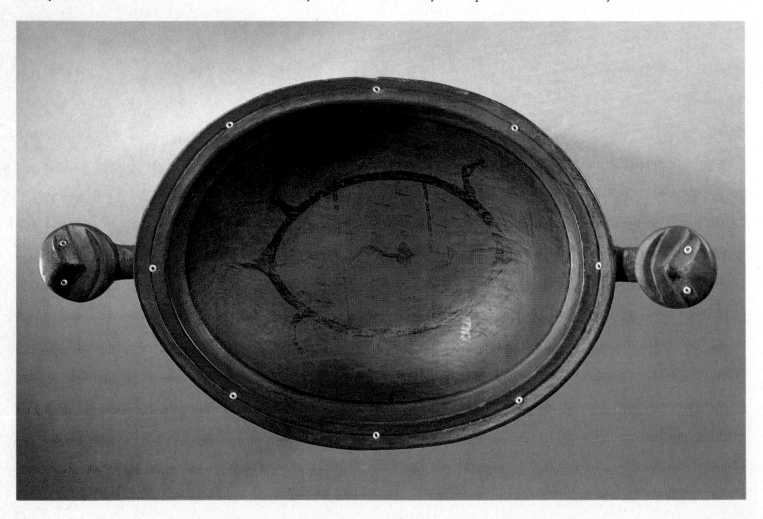

eyes and eyebrows. Widened eyes and raised eyebrows meant pleasure or affirmation, whereas narrowed eyes and lowered eyebrows – usually accompanied by a wrinkled nose and pursed lips – expressed displeasure or negation. This pattern prevailed in Greenland as in Alaska, more than a third of the way around the world.

Song was another major form of expression throughout the Eskimo area. It was always at hand, ready to burst forth in practically every circumstance. Eskimos sang to pass the time of day. They sang while they worked and while they danced. They played games with songs. They ridiculed each other with songs. They quieted distraught children with songs. They performed magic with songs. And they sang songs as part of their stories.

Eskimo singing had a tense, nasal quality. It was also characterized by a distinct throatiness, since the well-developed rhythm was controlled primarily by glottal pulsation (although often enhanced by use of a drum). To Western ears Eskimo singing had a harsh, strident sound, and the range and scale were quite narrow compared to Western music. When two or more people sang together they usually sang either in unison, or in unison at the octave; harmony was rarely a feature of Eskimo music. There was considerable variation from one region to another, however. As with other aspects of life, songs were generally more varied and complex among the Western Eskimos than among their Eastern relatives.

Eskimo songs dealt with almost every imaginable subject. Blood revenge, warfare, animals, love, hunting triumphs, human idiosyncrasies and tragedies, among other topics, served as subject matter. A verse from an Iglulik song about famine is typical:

Masks were used on humorous as well as serious occasions. This finger mask, with its leering face, was probably used during a song-dance performance intended to make the audience laugh.

> Hard times, dearth times
> Plague us every one.
> Stomachs are shrunken,
> Dishes are empty.
> Ayaa, yaa, yapape!
> Ayaa, yaa, yapape!

(Knud Rasmussen. *Intellectual Culture of Iglulik Eskimos. Report of the Fifth Thule Expedition 1921–24, Vol. VII, No. 1*, pp. 41–42, 1929.)

Some songs were of ancient origin and constituted part of the common cultural heritage of many different Eskimo groups. Others were composed for special events, and many were created spontaneously. Songs could be personal property, belong to certain families, or be the common property of an entire society. But songs of one kind or another were everywhere. When Rasmussen asked an Alaskan Eskimo how many songs he had composed, he replied, 'I merely know that I have many, and that everything in me is song. I sing as I draw breath.' (H. Ostermann & E. Holtved, eds. *The Alaskan Eskimos. Report of the Fifth Thule Expedition 1921–24, Vol. X, No. 3*, p. 137, 1952.)

Song frequently occurred together with dance. Among the Eastern Eskimos only one person – usually a man – normally danced at a time, and the dancer was usually also the drummer. He stood in one place in the middle of the room, knees bent, body hunched slightly forward. As he twisted the drum rhythmically back and forth to strike it on alternate sides, his body rose and fell in time to the music, and he swayed in a kind of semicircular motion from the hips. He might sing, at least at first, but song accompaniment was usually provided by the onlookers. Eyes shut, the drummer-dancer worked himself into an ecstatic state before exhaustion overcame him. At that point, he turned the instrument over to someone else and the performance would be repeated. In some areas partners danced and played drums together on festive occasions.

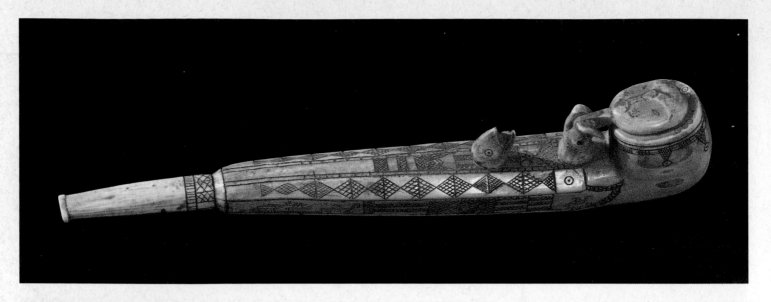

Left, above: This magnificent pipe from Point Hope, Alaska, was carved from walrus ivory. The bowl is capped with a female face, which could be flipped back when the pipe was in use. Walrus and polar bear heads are attached to the stem, which is incised with abstract designs.

Left, below: The rhythmic character of song was enhanced by the beating of a drum, the Eskimos' only musical instrument. This light West Alaskan hand drum was made of a shallow oval wooden frame covered on one side by a drumhead made from caribou stomach or intestines. It was held by the handle and struck on the underside by a long strip of wood manipulated so as to strike two parts of the frame simultaneously.

Below: Almost anything, in the right hands, could be made into an attractive object. This woman's belt is made of several dozen sets of caribou incisors, blue beads and the canine teeth of some large mammal, possibly a grizzly bear.

Among the Western Eskimos dancing was much more a group affair. There was also much greater variety and complexity in dance types. In Northwest Alaska, for example, they differentiated between fixed motion dances, free motion dances, sitting dances and kneeling dances. In a fixed motion dance, several people co-ordinated their movements with one another. Such dances were choreographed by a shaman or by a particularly adept dancer and taught to others. The fixed motion dance, although quite different in form, was analogous in concept to Western ballet or chorus dancing. The free motion dance, on the other hand, permitted almost as much variation as modern Western rock dancing. In both types of dance men and women danced differently. Men typically held themselves rigid. Knees bent, they moved about by jumping, and their arm and head movements were carried out in jerks. Women's dancing was much more graceful. Their feet remained on the floor, and, with eyes downcast, they kept time to the music by swaying their bodies, bending their knees and curving their arms. Sometimes women and men danced at the same time, sometimes not.

Sitting and kneeling dances, involving rhythmic movements of arms and head, were also found in Northwest Alaska. The former were performed mostly by women, the latter by men. In Southwest Alaska the men's kneeling dance was extremely common, and both men and women participated in sitting dances. Sitting dances could be performed in boats, where they frequently served as a form of diversion for people engaged in a long journey.

Eskimos, of course, danced for a variety of reasons. They danced in ceremonies, to pass the time, and for their own entertainment or for that of an audience. Dances for entertainment were often satirical: men would lampoon women's behaviour when picking berries, for example, or women would mimic the motions of a frustrated hunter. Almost as common were dances depicting stories and legends.

Dancing reached its greatest degree of development in the ceremonial context, and the most elaborate ceremonies were found in Alaska. One such dance was the wolf dance, which consisted of several episodes. In the first, three or four women and two men danced. The women held wands or rods decorated with feathers, and they did their typical swaying dance on one side of the floor, while on the other side, the men, wearing loon-skin head-dresses and long gauntlet

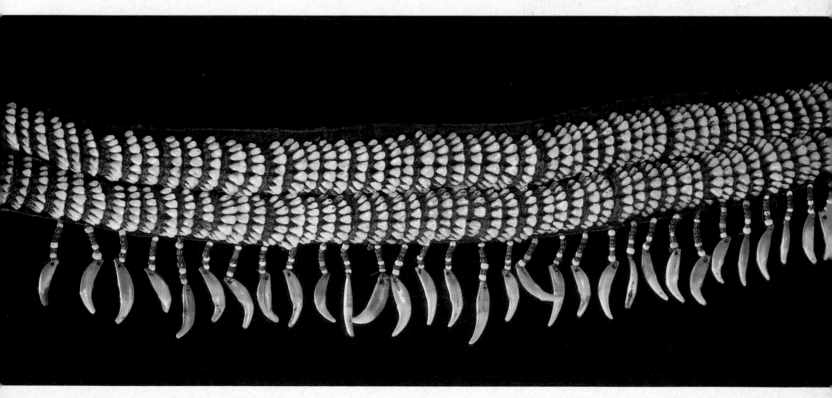

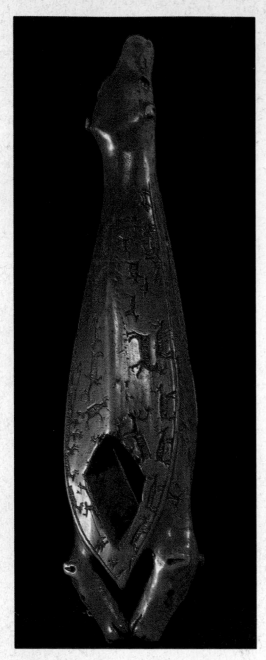

Above: Not content with making a mere arrow shaft straightener, the creator of this piece imbued it with both symbolism and beauty. Caribou, a major source of food, clothing and utensils, are seen both in the three heads at the ends of the tool and in many of the engravings spread over its surface. While being used to straighten arrows, it also massaged caribou souls, making the animals more amenable to being caught.

Right: Dancers often wore masks, which were frequently painted. Colours were derived from many sources – minerals, clay, soot, leaves, bark, roots, berry juice, grass and blood, each symbolizing a different quality. Inlaid ivory, beads, feather tassels and wooden appendages also were often employed, each of which also had magical or other symbolic significance. Many of these features are included in this masquette, which was worn on the forehead.

mittens, performed a pantomime dance expressing a wish to go outside. The mittens, and often the head-dresses, also served as rattles, small stones or bones, or perhaps amulets encased in membranes, being attached to them. The orchestra of perhaps three men playing frame drums and one man playing a box drum was seated to one side of the dance floor, and the audience was seated across from it. The fourth side of the dance floor was occupied by a screen symbolizing a wolf den.

The central episode began when a single male dancer wearing a wolf's-head mask and gauntlet rattle gloves performed a dance depicting the wolf character. Simultaneously, four similarly attired dancers enacted a complex series of manoeuvres and contortions behind the partially opened wolf den. They then emerged to dance on the main floor. During this part of the performance they conveyed gifts between different members of the audience, dancing all the while. When the gift distribution had been accomplished, they leapt backward, in unison, through small holes in the 'den' wall. As they disappeared, their masks and mittens were scraped off on to the floor.

The dance continued through several other episodes which differed in various respects from the two just described. At times the box drum alone provided the beat, while at others the frame drums, or the frame drums and the box drum together, did so. At times several people danced simultaneously, while at others the action involved just one or two people. Some of the dances required extremely vigorous dancing and extensive horizontal movement of both men and women, while others were quite sedate. The entire series was linked together in a precise sequence and took some five hours to complete.

The wolf's-head and loon masks used in the wolf dance were made of the skins of the wolf and loon respectively, but for most other Alaskan dances and ceremonies masks were made of wood. The creation and use of wooden masks was especially well developed in Southwest Alaska. In the Eastern Arctic masks were usually made of seal or caribou skin.

The creation of masks was only one form of traditional Eskimo art, a type of expression which permeated Eskimo material culture even more thoroughly than song pervaded their social life. Indeed, Eskimos did not differentiate between art and religious or utilitarian objects or decoration. All these elements were blended together in a single, cohesive whole.

Artefacts produced by Eskimos almost always exhibited an elegance and style far in excess of that demanded by the uses to which they were put. An ivory hairpin might terminate in the head of a walrus or seal, and be formed with a single graceful curve, or perhaps a series of sinuous curves, near one end; an ivory bodkin might be carved with undulating or notched sides, and be decorated with incised lines or dots; a wooden bag-handle might be shaped in the image of a polar bear. Fish-hooks, bags, needle-cases, toys, charms, combs, net-sinkers, dolls, bow-drills, knives, toggles, harpoon heads . . . all received artistic attention which elevated them above their mundane utilitarian purposes. And mundane, utilitarian purposes were all they were used for. A fine piece of craftsmanship would be noted and admired by everyone who saw it, but no one attempted to produce 'art' for the sake of exhibition; that came only with European influence. Traditional Eskimo art was purely expressive in nature. Its essence was the act of creation, not the object which resulted.

Even the human body was decorated – with tattoos, and with ear, nose, hair and lip ornaments, the precise list varying from one region to another. Many of these decorations – perhaps most of the ones representing animals – also served as charms. But Eskimos did not distinguish between the sacred and the profane, for every object had a spirit of its own, and every act, no matter what its purpose, was observed and reacted to by some spirit or other.

Practically every man and woman was an artist. The main materials they worked with were ivory, bone, caribou antler, skins and fur. In Southwest

Alaska there was considerable work in wood as well, not only in the creation of masks, but also in the making or decorating of paddles, rattles, boxes, bowls, graveyard effigies and monuments, sunshade hats, goggles to prevent snow blindness, and large hunting hats with carved charms – all painted with meaningful personal designs. There, and in the Pacific Eskimo and Aleut areas, they also did a great deal of work with grass, particularly in making exquisite baskets.

Quite a different sort of art form which attained a high level of development was storytelling. Eskimo tales were based on a rich body of folklore and historical tradition supplemented by the actual experiences and observations of the narrators themselves. They were expressed in a language which, despite its regional variations, was as rich as any other in concepts dealing with natural phenomena, sentiments, ideas, and the experiences of daily life. Eskimo languages are even more amenable than most to expressing subtle shades of meaning. This ability derives from what is sometimes referred to as their 'synthetic' structure. Most Eskimo words consist of a base to which is added one or more suffixes. Each suffix modifies to some extent not only the meaning of the base, but also both the individual and combined meanings of the suffixes previously attached to it. Thus *inuk*, 'human being', can become *inurujuk*, 'big human being', *inurujuksuaq*, 'a giant', *inurujuksuaqasik*', 'a cruel giant'.... Since there are hundreds, perhaps thousands of suffixes, and since several of them may be included within a single word, the number of variations in meaning resulting from the possible combinations is very large, if not incalculable.

Among the Western Eskimos and Aleuts, men always wore gloves when dancing, for reasons no one seems to recall. These long Aleut gauntlet gloves, made of sealskin with puffin beaks attached by short cords, also served as rattles when shaken in time to the beating of a drum.

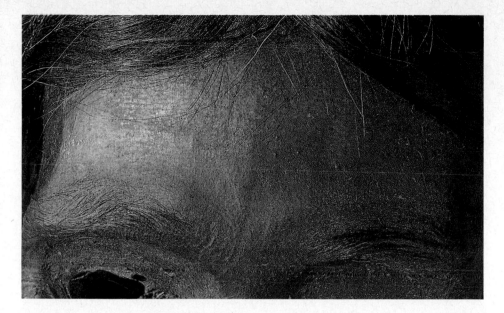

Linguistic ability varied from one person to another, of course. Some people could speak more eloquently than others, and some could master the large repertoire of stories better than others. The master storytellers who played such an important part in Eskimo life possessed not only eloquence and excellent memories, but also a great sense of showmanship. Stories were accompanied by animated facial expressions and gestures, and often by singing and dancing as well. A master could hold an audience's rapt attention for several hours a day, for several days or even weeks at a time. Among the Western Eskimos, some stories took all the evenings for four or five weeks to tell in their entirety.

The subject matter of Eskimo stories included almost every phenomenon within their experience. Since the Eskimo world view incorporated dreams, fantasies and external phenomena within a single sphere, the range of experience was very broad indeed. Actual events, views of nature, warfare, vengeance, human weakness, animals, interpersonal relations, epic tales and fantastic creatures were all part of the standard fare. Some of these characteristics are evident in the following short story from Baffin Island, in the eastern Canadian Arctic:

There were four men who went hunting together. Three of them were brothers, while the fourth one had taken their sister as wife. They went out to the floe-edge. Suddenly the ice broke away, and carried them out of sight of land. After some time the floe of ice became smaller and smaller. Then the oldest brother, who was a great [shaman], summoned his guardian spirit, a large bear, and told him of their plight. Then the ice floe began to tip up, and when it became quite steep, the oldest brother slid off in to the sea. When he came up again, he was transformed into a [polar] bear. The other brothers followed his example, and when they came up were also transformed into bears. Then they swam to the shore. The oldest brother told the other men that if they should see any seals, they must not kill them, else they would not regain their human shape. The brother-in-law could not resist the temptation of killing a seal when he saw it, and he devoured it. When they reached the land the oldest brother transformed himself into a gull, and flew to a place where the [people] were cutting up a whale. He had some of the meat, and took some back to his brothers. Then the brothers resumed human shape, but the brother-in-law had to remain a bear.

(Franz Boas, 'The Eskimo of Baffin Land and Hudson Bay'. *Bulletin of the American Museum of Natural History* Vol. XV, Pt. I, p. 326–327, 1901.)

In western Alaska men consumed tobacco primarily by smoking it in pipes, but women chewed it or took it as snuff. This snuff box is carved in the form of two seals — evidently a mother and its offspring, the smaller one serving as the removable lid. Incised lines and inset ivory and white bead pegs decorate the surface.

Aleuts divided their stories into three basic categories: myths and legends, epic tales about ostensibly historical people or events, and narratives about the past or present life of the Aleuts. Stories in the first group were regarded as essentially imaginary, those in the third as being definitely true, and those in the second as being some combination of the two. In Northwest Alaska and in the Eastern Arctic, stories were considered to be either true or mythical. In the Central Arctic, however, such distinctions seem not to have been made at all. Stories were thought to be true, no matter how fantastic they might appear to an outsider.

Stories were the primary medium whereby the common traditions of Eskimo culture, as well as of each individual society, were preserved and passed down

through the generations. They were sources of much practical information, such as how to hunt seals, and served to convey or reinforce ethical standards. Stories also constituted a major form of entertainment during long winter nights. In this capacity they held more or less equal rank with singing, dancing, and playing games.

A complete listing of Eskimo games would require a book in itself. There was a wide array of children's games, and a number of the games for people of all ages that are known in many parts of the world, such as blind man's buff, keep-away, hide-and-seek, tag, jump-rope, and 'monkey in the middle'. They also played a game similar to rounders (American 'baseball'), and another that was similar to football (American 'soccer'). Other familiar games in Alaska were the tug-of-war, top-spinning, juggling games, games similar to quoits, and various stick

Beautiful clothing was made from carefully selected furs from different animals or from different parts of the same animal. This elegant woman's parka from western Alaska was made from dozens of ground-squirrel skins shaped and pieced together, decorated with strips of white caribou hide and trimmed with pieces of wolf and wolverine fur.

games similar to jackstraws. In parts of Southwest Alaska they apparently even played games similar to ice-hockey and field-hockey.

A distinctive Alaskan game, much favoured at summer festivals, was the 'blanket toss'. A large, circular blanket would be made out of several walrus hides sewn together, with holes for hand-grips cut all around the edge. A dozen or more people held the blanket, and one person got on it. When the blanket was suddenly pulled taut, he would fly into the air. An expert at the game – young women were the best – could fly up more than ten metres (thirty-three feet) and perform a variety of twists and somersaults while in the air.

They also possessed a group of three games which, while individually by no means unique to them, might be considered a distinctively Eskimo grouping because they were played so frequently in so many areas. These included 'cup and ball', 'ring and pin', and 'cat's cradles'. In the first a spike was attached by means of a string to the shoulderblade of some small animal. The latter had several holes drilled through it, usually in a graded series of sizes. The player held the spike, swung the 'target' bone outwards and upwards, and attempted to thrust the spike through one of the holes. The smaller the hole, the higher the score. In the ring and pin game a target ('ring') of bone was suspended from the ceiling, and several players simultaneously attempted to thrust darts through holes drilled in it. Cat's cradles involved the manipulation of a string loop into a series of designs or figures. The Eskimos knew literally hundreds of them; each had a special name, and many were accompanied by special songs or stories. All three games could be played by a small and variable number of people in a restricted amount of space. Like storytelling and singing, they were enjoyed even in the smallest house during the longest winter night or in the very worst storm.

Important in the Yupik area were storyknife drawings that children, especially girls, made on snow, sand or mud. Made with an ivory knife, drawings of familiar objects and scenes might be accompanied by a story.

Games, of course, like other activities, were subject to taboos. Some could not be played by certain people, or at particular times of day or year, for fear of offending some spirit or other. But the overall repertoire was so large that at least some games could be enjoyed at any time.

Contests of strength and agility also held a prominent position in Eskimo recreational activities. In addition to foot races, jumping contests and wrestling bouts, which had to be performed out of doors, many could be carried out inside, some of them, like finger-pulling, arm-wrestling, ear-pulling and leg-wrestling, in a very small amount of space.

The Eskimos also had some interesting and difficult indoor jumping games. For example, in the two-legged high kick, the jumper had to strike with both feet simultaneously an object suspended from the ceiling and land back on the floor on both feet. No one knows how high people were able to jump in traditional times, but in some of the contests held in the 1970s men were successfully hitting targets nearly three metres (ten feet) above the floor, and women exceeded the two-metre (six-and-a-half-foot) mark. There was also a one-legged high kick, a two-legged back kick in which the goal was to strike with both feet an object suspended behind the jumper's back, and a lying down kick in which a person lying on the floor tried to strike a suspended object with his feet. Vigorous games such as these provided diversion for the entire community, and enabled hunters to keep in good condition even when bad weather kept them indoors.

Another form of recreation, particularly among the Eastern Eskimos, was group sex. Eskimo men did not lend their wives to strangers, but men and women sometimes did exchange spouses with good friends for a night or two, particularly when they were confined indoors for a prolonged period by winter darkness or stormy weather. In East Greenland they played a game called 'putting out the lamps'. Several couples congregated in one house, the lamps were extinguished, and everyone groped around in the dark for a member of the

Above: Before European trade goods reached the Eskimo area all their beads were made from bone or ivory, such as this ivory bead or pendant. Found on Ellesmere Island, in far northern Canada, it is carved in semi-human form. Judging from its shape, it may depict a woman wearing the long polar bear skin leggings characteristic of the Polar Eskimos.

Right: Traditional Eskimo carvings were small. They were meant to be held in the hand, suspended from the neck or attached to clothing, not placed on a shelf or table for display. One experienced them tactually and spiritually as much as visually. This small ivory carving of a human adorned with blue beads probably served as a charm, and hung by a cord from its owner's neck.

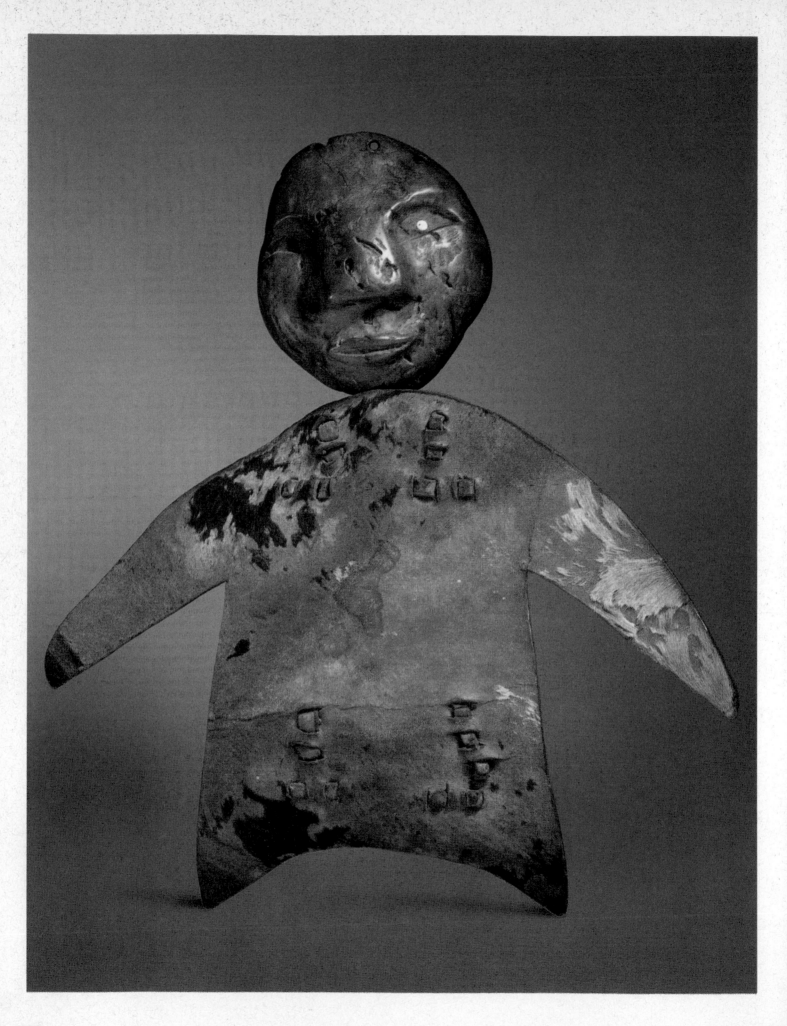

opposite sex. Sexual partners for the night would be whoever happened to end up together. Neither co-marriage nor incest rules apparently applied in this context. Sexual licence was more limited among the Western Eskimos, where sex has never been reported as a group activity.

The Eskimos' genius for coping with the harsh northern environment was exhibited perhaps most clearly in the way they spent the time between late November and early January. This is the time of long nights and short days; above the Arctic Circle, it is a time of no sun at all. Eskimos confronted this problem directly by turning what could have been the most miserable time of year into the holiday and festival season. It was the time when the most elaborate dances, games, ceremonies, festivals and feasts of the entire year were held.

The ability of Eskimos to cope, and even thrive, in regions most Westerners regard as uninhabitable has excited the admiration of everyone who has studied them. No matter how difficult the problem, they somehow found a solution. If their country lacked wood to make a sled, they carved and shaped dozens of pieces of ivory, lashed them together to make serviceable runners, crosspieces and stanchions, built their sled, and went about their business. If they lacked both wood and ivory, they rolled up some sealskins, soaked them in water, shaped them, froze them, lashed them together like so many pieces of wood, and proceeded on their way. If they lacked wood for fuel they burned seal oil; if they lacked seal oil they used fish oil; and if they lacked even that it didn't matter – they liked raw meat anyway. If their country was without wood and sod to use as building materials, they used stone and bone; if they had no stone or bone either, they constructed their dwellings out of snow. Nothing seemed to stop them.

The Eskimos' ingenuity and resourcefulness in technological matters was recognized and admired by even the most bigoted of the early European explorers and missionaries. What has taken much longer for Westerners to understand are the less tangible aspects of their traditional culture – the complexity of their family life, the wealth of their oral traditions, the beauty of their dances, the subtlety of their ideas, the breadth of their emotions. These reveal not the carefree, simple folk of Western lore, but an intelligent, complex, proud and sometimes even arrogant people, a people who survived more than 4000 winters in a land where few other groups could last even one.

Left: This Asiatic Eskimo puppet was made from driftwood and sealskin, with trade beads for eyes. It was probably used either as a child's toy or in humorous performances.

Below: Sexual symbolism was present but not particularly common in Eskimo art, despite the prevalence of sex as a subject of conversations and stories. However, the inside of the lid of this trinket box from Southwest Alaska is painted with several sexually explicit displays, as well as with pictures of animals, supernatural beings and hunting scenes.

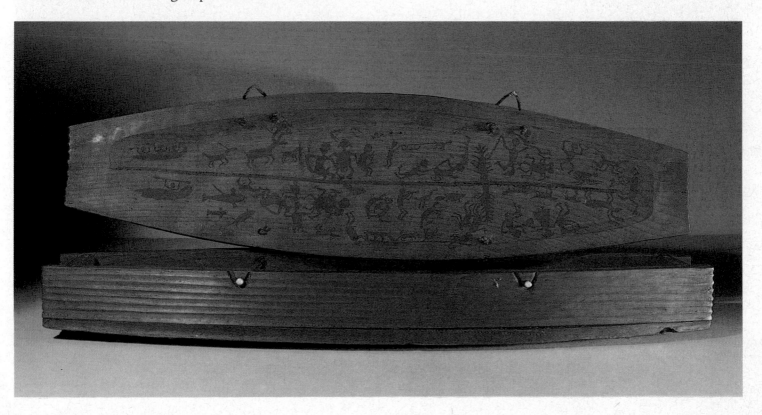

BIBLIOGRAPHY

Jennifer Ann, a two-year-old Baffin Island girl, looks out on a world that differs profoundly from the one her ancestors knew. Dressed here in a caribou-skin outfit, she will soon shift to a more Western style of clothing as she attempts to grapple with the new realities of northern life.

Briggs, Jean L., *Never in Anger: Portrait of an Eskimo Family*, Harvard University Press, Cambridge, Mass, 1970

Bruemmer, Fred, *Seasons of the Eskimo: A Vanishing Way of Life*, McClelland and Stewart, Toronto and Montreal, 1971

Burch, Ernest S., Jr (Compiler) *Peoples of the Arctic* [map], National Geographic Society, Washington, D.C., 1983

Carpenter, Edmund, Frederick Varley and Robert Flaherty, *Eskimo*, University of Toronto Press, Toronto, 1959

Curtis, Edward S., *The Alaskan Eskimo*, privately printed in 1930. Reprinted by Johnson Reprint Corporation, New York, 1970

Damas, David (ed.) *Handbook of North American Indians*, Volume 5, *Arctic*, Smithsonian Institution, Washington, D.C., 1984

Dumond, Don, *The Eskimos and Aleuts*, Thames and Hudson, London, 1977

Fitzhugh, William W. and Susan A. Kaplan, *Inua. Spirit World of the Bering Sea Eskimo*, published for the National Museum of Natural History by the Smithsonian Institution Press, Washington, D.C., 1982

Giddings, J. Louis, *Ancient Men of the Arctic*, Alfred A. Knopf, New York, 1967

Hughes, Charles Campbell, 'Under Four Flags: Recent Culture Change Among the Eskimos', *Current Anthropology*, Volume 6, no. 1, pp. 3–69, 1965

Jenness, Diamond, *The Life of the Copper Eskimos*, Report of the Canadian Arctic Expedition 1913–18, Volume XII, The King's Printer, Ottawa, 1922

Kleivan, I. and B. Sonne, *Eskimos. Greenland and Canada*, E.J. Brill, Leiden (Iconography of Religions, Section VIII, Fasc. 2), 1985

Laughlin, William S., *Aleuts: Survivors of the Bering Land Bridge*, Holt, Rinehart and Winston, New York, 1980

Nelson, Edward William, *The Eskimo About Bering Strait*, Eighteenth Annual Report of the Bureau of American Ethnology, 1896–97, Government Printing Office, Washington, D.C., 1899. Reprinted and republished, with an Introduction by William Fitzhugh, by Smithsonian Institution Press, Washington D.C., 1983

Nelson, Richard K., *Hunters of the Northern Ice*, The University of Chicago Press, Chicago and London, 1969

Oswalt, Wendell H., *Eskimos and Explorers*, Chandler and Sharp, Novato, California, 1979

Rasmussen, Knud, *Across Arctic America: Narrative of the Fifth Thule Expedition*, G. P. Putnam's Sons, London, 1927

Ray, Dorothy Jean and Alfred A. Blaker, *Eskimo Masks: Art and Ceremony*, University of Washington Press, Seattle and London, 1967

Vahl, M. *et al.* (eds.), *Greenland*. Volume II. *The Past and Present Population of Greenland*, C. A. Reitzel, Copenhagen, 1928

Weyer, Edward M., *The Eskimos: Their Environment and Folkways*, Yale University Press, 1932

INDEX

Numbers in italics refer to captions for illustrations

ACKNOWLEDGEMENTS

Werner Forman and the publishers would like to acknowledge
the help of the following in permitting the photography shown
on the pages listed:
Alaska Gallery of Eskimo Art: 20 bottom, 35, 58, 99, 102,
112 top, 121. Anchorage Museum of History and Art: 26 left, 64,
105. Edmund Carpenter: 22 right, 81 bottom. William Channing:
27, 31, 46, 56, 122. Eugene Chesrow: 49. Eugene Chesrow Trust:
103. The Danish National Museum: 19, 21 right, 101. Eskimo
Museum, Churchill, Canada: 45, 109. Field Museum of Natural
History, USA: 32 bottom, 54, 57, 76, 96. The Greenland
Museum: 11, 47, 48, 77, 78, 79 bottom, 82, 85, 86 top, 117.
Manitoba Museum of Man and Nature: 60, 70. Museum of
Mankind, London: 23, 24, 30, 59 right, 61, 63, 66, 67, 71 top and
bottom, 87, 90, 113, 114, 120. Sheldon Jackson Museum: 91, 97,
115. Jeffrey R. Myers Collection: 13, 33, 51, 55, 59 left, 75. The
Smithsonian Institution: 17 bottom, 29 left and right, 36, 37, 38,
39, 53 right, 62, 65, 74, 79 top, 80, 81 top, 83, 86 bottom, 92, 93,
94, 96, 104, 110, 112 bottom, 116, 118, 119, 123. Gallery
Tambaran: 26 right. George Terasaki: 89.

Werner Forman would also like to thank the following for their
help:
Claus Andreasen, Director, The Greenland Museum; Jørgen
Meldgaard, Director, The Danish National Museum; Susan
Rowley, Candace Greene, Joseph S. Brown, The Smithsonian
Institution; Peter L. Corey, Sheldon Jackson Museum; Walter A.
Van Horn, Curator, Anchorage Museum of History and Art;
Ronald Weber, James W. VanStone, Chairman, Field Museum of
Natural History, USA; Lorraine Brondson, Curator, Eskimo
Museum, Churchill; Dr E. Leigh Syms, Douglas Leonard,
Manitoba Museum of Man and Nature; Malcolm McLeod,
Director, Museum of Mankind, London; Edmund Carpenter.

Ernest S. Burch, Jr would like to thank the following for
suggestions, information or other assistance:
Lydia Black, Lisa Commager, Don Dumond, Michael Krauss,
Igor Krupnik, Susan Rowley, James W. VanStone, and especially
Margaret Lantis.

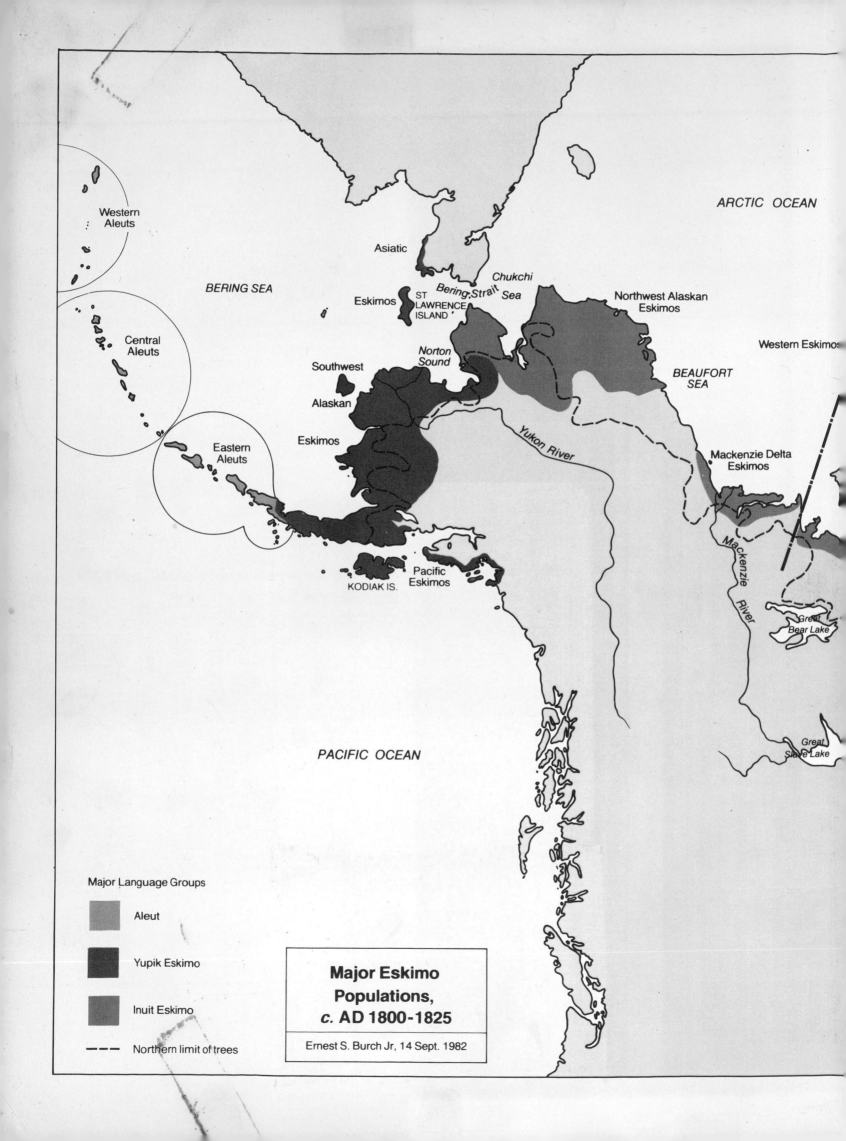

Major Language Groups

Aleut

Yupik Eskimo

Inuit Eskimo

--- Northern limit of trees

**Major Eskimo
Populations,
c. AD 1800-1825**

Ernest S. Burch Jr, 14 Sept. 1982

ARCTIC OCEAN

BERING SEA

Asiatic

Chukchi
Sea

Eskimos

Bering Strait

ST
LAWRENCE
ISLAND

*Norton
Sound*

Northwest Alaskan
Eskimos

Western Eskimos

*BEAUFORT
SEA*

Southwest

Alaskan

Eskimos

Mackenzie Delta
Eskimos

Yukon River

Western
Aleuts

Central
Aleuts

Eastern
Aleuts

Pacific
Eskimos

KODIAK IS.

PACIFIC OCEAN

*Mackenzie
River*

*Great
Bear Lake*

*Great
Slave Lake*